ARCHAEOLINGUA

Edited by
ERZSÉBET JEREM and WOLFGANG MEID

Series Minor
37

For my sons, Márton, Károly and János

ANDRÁS PATAY-HORVÁTH

THE ORIGINS OF THE OLYMPIC GAMES

BUDAPEST 2015

The publication of this volume was generously supported by the
Hungarian Scientific Research Fund
(Országos Tudományos Kutatási Alapprogramok, OTKA OT 101755)

Published in cooperation with the Institute of Archaeology at
the Research Centre for the Humanities of the Hungarian Academy of Sciences

Front Cover
The lower course of the Alpheios (photo: Ridi Graz)

Back Cover
Geometric bovine figurine from Greece (New York, Metropolitan Museum)

ISBN 978-963-9911-72-7

HU-ISSN 1216-6847

© by the author and Archaeolingua Foundation

All rights reserved. No part of this publication may be reproduced, stored in a retrieval system,
or transmitted in any form or by any means, electronic, mechanical, digitised, photocopying,
recording or otherwise without the prior permission of the publisher.

2015

ARCHAEOLINGUA ALAPÍTVÁNY
H-1250 Budapest, Úri u. 49.

Desktop editing and layout by Rita Kovács

Printed by Prime Rate Kft.

Contents

Preface 7

Photo Credits 9

Introduction: A Brief History of Research 11

A Ritual Parallel 17

The Archaeological Record of the 8th Century BC 21
    Tripod Cauldrons 21
    Animal Figurines 30

Making Sense of the Evidence 47
    The Archaeological Material 47
    The Basic Features of the Olympic Games 60
    Ritual Prescriptions 62
    The Penteteric Periodicity 66

Pelops and the Origins of the Games 75

Conclusion 93

Appendices 95
  I.   The Staphylodromia 95
  II.   Greek Geometric Bull Figurines Outside Olympia,
        the Kabeirion and Crete 100
  III.   Biological and Ethological Characteristics of Wild
        and Feral Bovines 102
  IV.   Aurochs and Wild Cattle in the Ancient Mediterranean 106
  V.   The Extinction of the Aurochs in Europe 114
  VI.   The Camargue Horses and Bulls 117
  VII. Basic Features of Hunting 119
  VIII. Prescriptions and Rituals Surrounding Hunting 122
  IX.   The Cult of Artemis at Geometric Olympia 125
  X.   Ethnographic Parallels for Pelops and Hippodameia 129

Abbreviations 133

Bibliography 135

Index of Ancient Passages Cited 153

Preface

> "one should disregard the ancient stories both of the founding of the sanctuary and of the establishment of the games ... for such stories are told in many ways, and no faith at all is to be put in them"
> (Strabo, *Geogr.* 8.3.30, English translation by H. Jones)

Although nowadays Olympia is generally connected with its famous athletic contests, this was originally not the case and it is by no means evident why the famous games were established here at an early date, which is traditionally referred to as 776 BC. The archaeological record shows beyond reasonable doubt that during the Early Iron Age the sanctuary existed and flourished for a long time without the games and there is nothing to prove that it would have been established originally or primarily to house sports events. Even after the games became popular, the sanctuary remained an important location for victory monuments celebrating military successes.

It was controversial already in antiquity, when and why the Olympic Games were established and by whom. Modern scholarship has also advanced a great number of hypotheses on the origins of the games, but a really convincing reconstruction has not been formulated yet. Admittedly, the subject is a very complex one. Different kinds of evidence should be treated cautiously and related problems can only be dealt with in a monograph which is, however, apart from a rather problematic one, missing so far. The present volume seeks therefore to fill this gap by presenting a new overall explanation for the phenomenon. This explanation is admittedly a hypothetical one, based mainly on the interpretation of the archaeological material and some ethnographic parallels, but due to the complete absence of contemporary written evidence, it cannot be otherwise. And although it is essentially a simple one, it must remain, as with any other previous similar theory, beyond definitive proof. And although it seems to the present author a fairly probable one, it is meant to further the discussion and "any who raise complaint have an easy remedy: to offer something better, something coherent and constructive."

One question which was frequently discussed in previous scholarship, i.e. the reliability of the traditional foundation date 776 BC, is completely and deliberately left out of consideration here, because it seems quite obvious (at least to the present author), that during the Early Iron Age, no single decisive foundation could have taken place. The date was established or calculated, as is well-known, only centuries later, and there is no hope of retrieving the exact methods or principles underlying it. Anyway, one can safely assume that all the dates appearing in our sources are artificial ones and, similarly to the many myths surrounding the foundation of the Olympic Games, it is not particularly likely that they would directly reflect historical reality. Instead of a single foundation date, a period of formation is more likely and can certainly be dated, even if only in an approximate manner, to the Early Iron Age including the Protogeometric, Geometric and Early Archaic periods and ranging in terms of absolute chronology approximately from the 10th to the 7th century BC.

Instead of debating or searching for the exact date, it is more important and more interesting, I think, to reconstruct the way in which the games were established and the circumstances, which allowed or caused their widespread and early popularity as well as the high prestige attached to them.

After having clarified the title and the scope, it remains to acknowledge the help of many institutions and persons to whom I am greatly indebted. The basic idea came during a research stay at the Freie Universität, Berlin, financed by the Alexander von Humboldt Foundation. During the past two years, the substantial financial support of the Hungarian National Research Fund (OTKA ref. no. 101755) and the János Bolyai postdoctoral fellowship provided by the Hungarian Academy of Sciences contributed in many different ways to elaborate the theory presented here.

I greatly benefited from the advice, comments and encouragement of Gy. W. Hegyi, Zs. Simon, L. Bartosiewicz, P. Siewert, M. Kiderlen, S. Lewis, W. Puchner and M. Golden. I have presented various parts of these ideas at different venues and received some valuable comments from the audiences at Budapest, Berlin, Paris, Pécs and Edinburgh. The feedback from different renowned journals and anonymous reviewers rejecting earlier drafts of some chapters also helped to elaborate the argument, and I take this opportunity to express my gratitude to all of them.

Photo Credits

Fig. 1. Bronze bovine figurines found at Kato Syme,
Crete: Schürmann 1996 no. 274, 320, 321, 463
© Deutsches Archäologisches Institut, Athen
(neg. 1997/ 391, 1487, 2023, 2043) 34

Fig. 2. Bronze bovine figurines found at Olympia:
B 1346, 1695, 2399, 4329, 5149 Br. 204, 1990, 2208, 9192, 9871,
10808, K 882, 899 © Deutsches Archäologisches Institut, Athen
(neg. 69/377, 380, 423, 448, 449, 469, 475, 70/623, Ol. 1761, 7233,
7243, 7264, 7270); skeleton of an aurochs: Copenhagen Nat. Mus.
ZMK 9/1864 (courtesy of the museum) 48

Fig. 3. Bronze bull figurine from the Theban Kabeirion, ca. 6th century BC.
New York, Metropolitan Museum 20.210
(http://www.metmuseum.org/collection/the-collection-online/
search/250963) 49

Fig. 4. Bronze bovine figurines found at Olympia
(after FURTWÄNGLER 1890); feral cattle from the Camargue
(http://www.saintesmaries.com/en/assets/images/
diapos/taureaux/t03.jpg) 52

Fig. 5. Geometric bovine figurines from Greece:
Baltimore, Walters Art Gallery 54. 2379 (http://art.thewalters.org/
detail/2048/geometric-statuette-of-a-bull); New York,
Metropolitan Museum 1972.118.82 (http://www.metmuseum.org/
collection/the-collection-online/search/255395) 101

Fig. 6. The characteristic position of aurochs horns
(after VAN VUURE 2005, fig. 21) 103

Fig. 7. Comparison of aurochs and domestic cattle
(after VAN VUURE 2005, fig. 16) 104

Fig. 8. Interior of building VI.A.8 from Çatalhöyük
(after MELLAART 1967, fig. 42) 106

Fig. 9. Golden vessel from Ugarit and stone relief from Alaca Höyük
(after VON LENGERKEN 1955, figs. 93, 100) 107

Fig. 10. Late Cypriot ivory gaming box from Enkomi (tomb no. 58).
ca. 1250–1050 BC.; London BM GR 1897.0401.996.
© Trustees of the British Museum 109

Fig. 11. Stone reliefs from Zincirli and Tell Halaf
(after VON LENGERKEN 1955, figs. 95, 97) 109

Fig. 12. Relief from the North West Palace at Nimrud (Kalhu).
Royal bull hunt of Ashurnasirpal II (875-860 BC).
London BM 124532. © Trustees of the British Museum 109

Fig. 13. Bronze reliefs from the Idaean Cave (Crete)
(after VON LENGERKEN 1955, figs. 111–112.) 110

Fig. 14. Sarcophagus relief from Golgoi (Cyprus). ca. 475–450 BC.
New York, Metropolitan Museum 74.51.2451
(http://www.metmuseum.org/collection/the-collection-online/
search/242004) 110

Fig. 15. Wild bull dragged to a ship. Detail of the late Roman mosaic floor
of the villa at Piazza Armerina. (© José Luiz Bernardes Ribeiro /
Wikimedia commons / CC-BY-SA-4.0) 111

Fig. 16. The decline of the last aurochs population
in the forests of Jaktorow, Poland
(after VAN VUURE 2005, fig. 11) 115

Introduction: a Brief History of Research

It is generally and most probably correctly assumed that the sanctuary of Olympia was not a centre for athletic contests from the very beginning of its existence,[1] and it is therefore legitimate to ask why it became the earliest and most important location for carrying out sport festivals on a regular basis. The question was formulated already in antiquity and several different answers were proposed by ancient and modern commentators alike, but a really convincing explanation is still missing.[2]

Ancient literary sources considering the origins of the games are mainly mythological narratives involving different divine or heroic contestants and founders.[3] They might contain some elements reflecting the real historical developments, but without the aid of other sources, it is hard to decide which traits could be considered as such. So they are particularly ill-suited to start with and will be treated only at the end of this volume. The authenticity of the olympic victor lists is equally open to doubts,[4] but is in my view not to be dismissed entirely. Admittedly, the exact dates, names and origins of the earliest athletes are far from being sure, but the gradual development of the festival from simple origins to a complex event involving more and more types of races and contests is unanimously attested and may be realistic, since it is unlikely that a great local or supraregional festival would have been created suddenly, *ex nihilo*, in the Early Iron Age. Later on, the program was constantly changing, but never radically and this is only to be expected at the earliest stages as well. This does not mean that the ancient explanation given for this gradual development (Paus. 5.8.5) should be accepted at face value, but the evolution of the games as outlined by

---

[1] See most recently TAITA 2009 and SINN 2010.
[2] It was even stated by ULF – WEILER 1980, 31 in a more pessimistic way, that there is no way of unveiling the real origins of the games: "Gesetzt den Fall, eine Spekulation würde zufällig zur Formulierung der historisch zutreffenden Herkunftstheorie führen, sie ließe sich für uns als solche beim gegenwärtigen Stand der Quellen nicht erkennen." Despite this discouraging conclusion, a new hypothesis (to be discussed below) was nevertheless formulated (SIEWERT 1991, VALAVANIS 2006) and even ULF (1991, 25–30) admitted afterwards that the research is not necessarily bound to fail in this respect. The most recent treatment (INSTONE 2007) suggests not a single source for the origins of the Games, but tries to combine multiple causes, discussing earlier hypotheses, but offering nothing new beyond religion and politics.
[3] A convenient summary is given by Paus. 5.7.10 – 5.8.5. See also ULF 1997a.
[4] CHRISTESEN 2007.

the victor list is nevertheless a plausible one. It is still puzzling, however, that according to ancient tradition the games would have originally consisted only in a single stadion race, because this event is not a particularly exciting or spectacular one and it certainly seems to strain credulity, that people living far away from the sanctuary would readily have agreed to undertake a long and troublesome journey only to attend an event which takes some 30 seconds. Multiple contests were therefore assumed by various scholars, referring also to the complex games attested by Homeric epic.[5] The consideration addresses a real problem and is not to be dismissed entirely, but is hardly convincing in every respect. The assumption of some other events next to the stadion is actually a very attractive one, but there are also some serious objections against the hypothesis of early games in the Homeric fashion: it is hard to see why other contests, which were practised later and were even more popular than the stadion race would have been neglected in this way and it is equally unclear, why precisely the stadion race was selected as the most ancient game, if not for the simple reason, that this was really the case, since running events are certainly not very important in the games descibed in epic. In addition, the Homeric parallels were noticed in antiquity as well and it would have been quite easy to adjust the history of the Olympic Games in this sense, but this apparently never occurred as a means of solving the problem and the primacy and exclusivity of the stadion race was never questioned. This would be quite surprising, if the entire matter had been mere fiction. So it is reasonable to suppose that it was not only the stadion race, which attracted visitors from far away, but it is equally likely that the other events, which are not recorded by the literary tradition, were not those practised subsequently. This assumption is not as absurd as it seems at first, and a convenient suggestion will be made below, but ancient literary sources simply do not reveal any more about this matter.

Modern theories concerning the origins of the Olympic Games were discussed at length earlier,[6] but should be summarized here as well. The oldest

---

[5] GARDINER 1925, 87–88; HERRMANN 1972, 80–81. GOLDEN 1998, 39, 43–45 equally questions, for other reasons, that the stadion would have been originally the single contest and supposes that other disciplines, most importantly the chariot race was already introduced at an earlier date than traditionally assumed. This kind of reconstruction would mean an early and widespread popularity of the games, which seems to be unlikely given the complete silence of the epic tradition.

[6] ULF – WEILER 1980.

theory suggested that the games originated from funeral ceremonies[7], while the most widespread idea during the 20th century was that they were a test to select the best successor/ruler or a ritual contributing to maintain the energies of nature (vegetation magic/*hieros gamos*).[8] The most recent suggestion is that the games would have started from initiation ceremonies (*rites de passage*)[9] involving entire age-groups of young men.

All these traditional explanations started from various ancient myths concerning the origins of the games and combined them with ethnographic parallels and observations. Therefore, it is only natural that they arrived at widely different results, none of them being able to claim more plausibility than another.

Moreover, all these theories fail to explain and do not even address the question why it was precisely the sanctuary of Olympia where the games were established and why these games became so popular here at such an early date and failed to gain this prestige and popularity elsewhere. These two intimately interconnected questions are, however, fundamentally important and any serious reconstruction of the origins of the games should offer an answer to them.

Traditionally the reason for the choice of the site and for the rapidly growing popularity of the games is sought rather superficially in the cult of Zeus or more specifically in his oracle,[10] but actually it is by no means sure that the earliest cult was directed towards Zeus (female deities are amply attested later as well);[11] the first Doric temple was dedicated not to Zeus but Hera[12] and the early dedications do not attest beyond doubt that Zeus was the main god of the site) and the early establishment of his oracle is also open to doubts.[13] Even if the cult of Zeus and/

---

[7] Most prominently MEULI 1941 and 1968. Other works containing the same idea are discussed in detail by ULF – WEILER 1980, 2–15.

[8] COOK 1904; FRAZER 1911; VALLOIS 1926; CORNFORD 1927; DREES 1962. Cf. ULF – WEILER 1980, 15–20. An isolated attempt has also been made to trace the origins of the games to some unspecified harvest festival: SWADDLING 1980, 12.

[9] JEANMAIRE 1939, 413–418; BRELICH 1969, 449–456; BURKERT 1972, 108–119.

[10] SINN 1991.

[11] Pausanias mentions a cult place for Gaia (5.14.10), Eiliethyia (6.20.2), Meter Theon (5.20.9) and seven altars for Artemis (5.15.4–7; 5.18.8). See in general HERRMANN 1962.

[12] Most commentators today agree that originally the temple called Heraion by Pausanias (5.16.1) was built for the cult of Zeus, but see most recently PATAY-HORVÁTH 2013.

[13] According to Schol. Pind. *Ol.* 6.6, an ancestor of the seer Agesias participated in the foundation of Syrakousai and this piece of evidence supports the claim of WENIGER 1915, 68–72 and KETT 1966, 18–20, that Elean seers played an important part already

or his oracle were earlier than the games, this alone would hardly explain why the sanctuary attained a supraregional popularity during the Early Iron Age, since other cults of Zeus remained local and other supraregional sanctuaries did not host sport events until the beginning of the 6th cent. BC. either.

This observation would seemingly corroborate the view expressed by various scholars, that the athletic contests did not originate from a specific cult or ritual, but were entirely secular and attached only secondarily and mainly for practical reasons to sanctuaries.[14] The latter assumption is, however unsatisfactory for several reasons. It can hardly explain the choice of Olympia (which is conspicuously located far away from the main political centres and relatively densely populated regions of Early Iron Age Peloponnese), the exclusivity and the permanence of the site (other localities might have been favoured as well) and is especially unlikely given the fact that all major athletic games were closely linked to specific sanctuaries and cult festivals, even if a major *polis* responsible for organising them, could in theory have selected some other more convenient locations or timing.[15] Secular games in ancient Greece are rarely attested and certainly were *ad hoc* events, not recurring ones attracting competitors on a regular basis for a long time and from a wide region.

So the religious origins of the games seem to fit the available evidence much better[16] and will be retained here as a starting point as well. The most recent theory also started from this assumption and achieved a considerable advance in identifying the cultic origins of the games by using not some mythical tales, but a certain ritual, which is attested for Olympia.[17] Unfortunately, I think that even this

---

during the 8th cent. BC. Pindaros says, on the contrary only that it was Agesias himself, who participated in the foundation and it is more likely that this referred only to the refounding by Gelon (cf. WILAMOWITZ 1922, 307). The hypothesis formulated by the scholion is therefore a very dubious basis for theories concerning the early history of elean divination.

[14] GARDINER 1916–1918, 102–106. Further literature is given by ULF –WEILER 1980, 27–29.

[15] It was only the Nemean Games, which were transferred more than once to Argos (MILLER 1989, 61–62). The impractical location of the games is particularly clear at Delphi (on the steep slope of the mountain) and at Olympia lying some 50 km away from the *polis* Elis, which was responsible for organising the games for several centuries.

[16] GOLDEN 1998, 12–17, INSTONE 2007, 75–77 agree in this respect, although very cautiously. More sceptical is MURRAY 2014, 313 but she does not go into details.

[17] SIEWERT 1992, elaborated by VALAVANIS 2006.

hypothesis cannot represent a definitive explanation for the origins of the games, because the ritual attested by Philostratus is most probably an ancient fiction[18] and can therefore not be used to reconstruct historical reality. The relevant passage is the following one:

> „The single-stade dash competition was invented in this way. When the Eleans sacrificed, they placed offerings on the altar, but they did not light the fire. Runners took their place a stade from the altar and in front of the altar stood a priest with a torch, serving as a judge. The victor in the race set fire to the offerings and went away as an Olympic winner" (Philostr. Gymn. 5; English transl. by S. Instone)[19]

That the lighting of the sacrificial fire is not attested for any real Olympic victor is admittedly only an *argumentum e silentio*, even if it might seem a rather strong one, given the vast amount of information concerning the victors. But there is another similar problem as well. There were indeed athletes who were apparently involved in lighting the sacred fire on the altar, but only the winners of torch races.[20] This usage of a torch is natural enough, but the basic problem is that in Olympia, there were no torch races. Moreover, torch races were always carried out during the night, but in Olympia all the contests were strictly confined to daytime. So it is rather probable that there was no such race at the very beginnings of the games either. Philostratus (or his source) seems to have developed only a hypothesis, which was constructed on the basis of well-known torch races, but because this competition was not practised at Olympia, the torch was *faute de mieux* given to the priest acting as an equally hypothetical judge.

---

[18] INSTONE 2007, 78 soberly compares other similar explanations given by the same author, which are equally and most obviously fictive. See most recently CUCHE 2014, 18: „Encore une fois, il peut être dangereux de prendre Philostrate pour un historien Ce n'est pas que son aition soit sans valeur, bien au contraire : il en dit long sur l'imaginaire attaché à cette épreuve sportive ; mais ce n'est pas un document sur le premier siècle de l'olympisme, dont il faut bien admettre qu'on ne sait pas grand chose."

[19] The passage was also discussed by SANSONE 1988, 83; GOLDEN 1998, 19; SCANLON 2002, 35–36.

[20] There is epigraphical evidence for this custom at Delphi from the 2nd cent. BC (FD III 3 no. 238; SOKOLOWSKI 1962, no. 44: a race founded by Eumenes II. ca. 160–159 BC.) At the Panathenaic games the pyre was lit with the torch of the winner, but not necessarily by himself (cf. Schol. Plat. *Phaedr.* 231e and DEUBNER 1932, 211).

One is also wondering, why this hypothetical race could have become a great attraction and why it could rapidly gain wide popularity. It actually rather supposes a large number of candidates, but is not really capable of attracting them. Even if the adduced parallels[21] strongly suggest that the race was used, similarly to other rituals, to select the favourite of the gods, it is highly improbable that the goal of the race was simply to light the sacred fire.

Should we therefore conclude that there is apparently no ritual recorded by our extant sources, which could qualify as the predecessor of the Olympic Games? Should we either abandon the search for the precise cultic origins of the games or even accept the theory of purely secular origins? I think this would be unwise, because our possibilities are far from being exhausted: that a relevant ritual is not directly attested for Olympia does not mean that there was none, and since it is unlikely to have been an absolutely unique ritual, it is only to be expected that some parallels can be found outside Olympia, in some other Greek *pol(e)is* the citizens of which frequently visited the sanctuary and its games.

---

[21] SIEWERT 1992. The parallels are not compelling, because the winners are simply taking their share from the sacrifice, but are not active administrators of the sacrifice itself.

A Ritual Parallel

To start a search for parallels, one has first to define the characteristic features we are looking for in other rituals and/or festivals. The most conspicuous one is the importance attached to the footrace or a similar running event, but some kind of oracular function is likely to be equally important. Since the oracle practised at Olympia was specialised in military affairs,[22] a military aspect may also be supposed to have been present in a similar festival. The ritual must in addition have attracted a large number of wealthy people already during the 8th century BC, because the numbers of expensive votive dedications (tripod cauldrons) rapidly increase in this period and come from widely varying regions of the Peloponnese and even outside it. It is therefore likely to find a parallel ritual and/or festival in these particular regions, and it is only to be expected that it was a fairly important one. Furthermore, it is highly probable that similar festivals were celebrated at approximately the same period of the year, i.e. around July and August.[23]

Considering all these features, the Dorian Karneia[24] seem to be the best possible parallel for the Olympic Games. As the similarities have usually gone unnoticed,[25] it is appropriate to summarize and to discuss them briefly here.

First of all, a running event (the *stadion* race and the *staphylodromia*) had a prominent role in both.[26] Admittedly, the *staphylodromia* was, in contrast to the *stadion*, not a proper race, but merely the pursuit of a selected runner, but as the discussion below will show, this distinction between race and chase is not a particularly important one and the race is likely to have evolved from a ritual chase. The Karneia was regarded in antiquity as a *mimesis* of war camp (Athenaios 4.141e–f) and the outcome of the *staphylodromia* was explicitly

---

[22] SINN 1991, 2010.
[23] Schol. Pind. Ol. 3.35a. Cf. BELOCH 1913, 139–143; WENIGER 1905, 28–33; most recently ROBERTSON 2010, 66–67.
[24] The sources are collected and discussed in many different studies and handbooks, e.g. WIDE 1893, 73–86; NILSSON 1906, 118–129; BURKERT 2011, 354–358; PETTERSSON 1992, 57–72; ROBERTSON 2003, 36–74; SCULLION 2007, 193–196; DUCAT 2006, 274–277; CHRISTIEN – RUZÉ 2007, 14–16; RICHER 2009, 213–223; RICHER 2011, 423–456.
[25] They are briefly mentioned, as far as I can see, only in CORNFORD 1927, 233–235.
[26] The importance of the stadion is clearly shown by the fact that it was unanimously regarded as the most ancient game. The central role of the *staphylodromia* is not explicitly attested by ancient sources, but the fact that it has so many ethnographic parallels (WIDE 1893, 76–77), implies that it was the core of the festival. For further details cf. Appendix I.

regarded as a portent.[27] Moreover both festivals were celebrated at full moon[28] approximately in August or September, sometimes as in 480 BC exactly at the same time[29] and both were accompanied by a sacred truce.[30] The cult legends of both festivals centred around the figure of a seer (Karnos and Oxylos respectively) who played an active role in the return of the Heraclids.[31] Finally, the Karneia also shows a penteteric periodicity, because the *karneatai*, responsible for the organization and from whom the *staphylodromoi* were also selected, were in charge for four years.[32] Considering how little is known about the Karneia in general, the strong similarities cannot be regarded as incidental. In addition, the Karneia celebrating the alleged return of the Heraclids played an important role

---

[27] Bekker, anecd. 1. 305 s.v. *staphylodromoi*: καὶ ἐὰν μὲν καταλάβωσιν αὐτόν, ἀγαθόν τι προσδοκῶσι κατὰ τὰ ἐπιχώρια τῇ πόλει· εἰ δὲ μή, τοὐναντίον. The interpretative translation given by DUCAT 2006, 276: „good omen for the crops in the community's territory".

[28] This in itself is a rather peculiar feature, since there are few ancient Greek festivals which were tied to the full moon. Cf. also n. 177 below.

[29] The date is discussed in detail most recently by RICHER 2009, 219–221. It is not very likely that both festivals were regularly celebrated at the same full moon (although this is assumed by ROBERTSON 2003, 39), and that they coincided in 480 BC, can be rather seen as an exceptional case.

[30] For the date: Her. 7.208; for the truce at the Karneia: Thuk. 5.54 and 5.75.

[31] Karnos: Paus. 3.13.3-4; Oxylos: Paus. 5. 3-4. Strabo 8.3.30 p. 354 and Paus. 5.8.5 mention him as one of the mythical founders of the Olympic Games. The tales about Karnos and Oxylos are present as two consecutive episodes of the return of the Heraclids in Apollodorus Bibl. 2. 169–180, even if Karnos is not mentioned by name. In addition to the striking similarities of the myths, it is even possible that the two names have a similar meaning. The name of Oxylos was explained in different ways but the most recent discussion (MÜLLER-GRAUPA 1942, 2036–2038) refuted all earlier attempts and pleaded for the derivation from ὀξυδερκής. The main argument (and the only semantic one) was that Oxylos had three eyes. A more straightforward etymology, the derivation of the name from ὀξύς was already assumed by FICK-BECHTEL 1894, 225 and may refer to the horns, which most probably explain the name of Karnos as well (USENER 1913, 288–289 *pace* ROBERTSON 2003, 68–71, who seeks to derive the name of Karnos from κράνεια / κράνον, i.e. cornel tree or spear). Oxylos is not a real seer, even if he is certainly very similar to them in leading or guiding the advancing Dorians. Unlike seers, Oxylos is a murderer and also the son of Haimon and grandson or father of Andraimon (Apollodorus *Bibl.* 2.8.3). These „bloody" names also suggest that his name is not merely referring to the sharpness of his eyes, but has to be taken literally.

[32] Hesych. s.v. *karneatai*: ἐπὶ τετραετίαν ἐλειτούργουν.

in the Dorian ethnogenesis[33], while Olympia and its games were instrumental in forging a common Hellenic identity.[34]

Even if the similarities between Karneia and the Olympic Games are striking, the two festivals were celebrated not for the same god and it is perhaps precisely this difference, which prevented the recognition of the parallels. But actually Hesychius (s.v. *agetes*) attests that the Karneia was called at Sparta *agetoria* as well, the priest himself *agetes,* and that it was Zeus Agetor to whom Spartan kings sacrificed when departing to a military campaign. In addition, Karnos was called in Argos *Agetor* or even Zeus (Schol. Theokr. 5. 83b) and one can reasonably infer therefore that the festival was called there *agetoria* as well. This clearly shows the connection of the festival with Zeus and strongly suggests that the difference in the honoured god is not as decisive as it might seem at first.[35] On the other hand, the Olympic Games were also often celebrated in the month called Apollonios and if this is not totally accidental, it might suggest a connection with Apollon.[36]

As mentioned above, there seems to be a fundamental difference between the *staphylodromia* and the *stadion* at Olympia, because the first was a chase, the second one a race. The myth of Pelops and Oinomaos, however, clearly shows that this difference is not a particularly relevant one and the two kinds of contests were not strictly separated. The chariot race of Pelops and Oinomaos, as it is conventionally called, was actually a chase *par excellence*, but this did not prevent Pindar from using it without the need of any justification as an appropriate theme to celebrate a hippic victory. In the myth, the same principle can be observed as in the *staphylodromia*: if the pursued person is caught (and this seems to be generally the case), this success is a good omen, if on the contrary, the pursued person is able to escape, this is a complete disaster for his opponent or for the community. This similarity between the myth and the ritual strongly suggests that they have some common roots and since the *staphylodromia* has several ethnographic parallels[37], it is very likely to represent a ritual chase, from which the actual race, the *stadion* has evolved.

---

[33] ROBERTSON 1980; 2003.
[34] HALL 2002, 154–168.
[35] AUFFAHRT 1998, 488: „Zudem ist kaum ein Fest exklusiv nur mit einem Gott, umgekehrt sind Feste gleichen Typs mit unterschiedlichen Göttern verbunden."
[36] Schol. Pind. Ol. 3. 35a. Vgl. HANNAH 2005, 37–39.
[37] WIDE 1893, 76–77.

Our extant ancient sources certainly do not envisage any connection between the Karneia and the Olympic Games, and modern research has also failed to perceive and to explain the similarities. The parallels between the two rituals are however very pronounced and call, in my opinion, for some kind of reasonable explanation.

Since the athletic games and the sanctuary are not an exclusively Dorian establishment and there is no apparent reason why the Olympic Games should have influenced only the Dorians in such a way, it is unlikely, that the Karneia would have influenced the Olympic Games or *vice versa*. Some kind of common origin seems to be more plausible, but on the basis of the literary tradition alone, this is hard to identify. So it is time to turn our attention to the archaeological remains.

The Archaeological Record of the 8th Century BC

Tripod Cauldrons

The sanctuary of Olympia has produced by far the largest number of geometric tripod cauldrons and also a considerable number of similar cauldrons on conical or rod stands with orientalizing decor from the following century. The material was meticulously published by various German archaeologists and therefore the dating and to a great extent the localization of the production centres are clear enough: the stylistic affinities clearly show that the tripod cauldrons date from ca. 900 (or possibly even 1000) to 700 BC, while the orientalizing cauldrons start from the last quarter of the 8th and continue to the first quarter of the 6th; they were not manufactured by local bronzesmiths but by those from Laconia, Argolid, Corinth, and Attica. The only uncertainty in this respect is whether it was the products or perhaps in some cases the producers who actually travelled to Olympia.[38] Their distribution, parallels, and stylistic affinities have been studied from different perspectives,[39] but their interpretation, their social, historical, and religious context is still debated and requires an in-depth investigation. Fortunately, there are a few basic facts in this respect as well, which are beyond doubt: the tripod cauldrons and their successors are (1) prestige objects of extremely high material value (2) and were offered as votives in the Olympic *altis* as in many other sanctuaries but (3) in a far greater number than anywhere else.[40] The open questions can be formulated in an equally simple way: (1) Who were the dedicators? (2) Which god was or which god(desse)s were honoured? (3) What was the occasion on which the cauldrons were dedicated?[41]

---

[38] FURTWÄNGLER 1890 (esp. Nr. 544–641 with Taf. 27–33); WILLEMSEN 1957; MAASS 1978; HERRMANN 1966; 1979. For the traditional chronology of the earliest pieces see MAASS 1978, 228, revised by JANIETZ 1989, 18–20 and KIDERLEN 2010, 98–102.

[39] BENTON 1935; SCHWEITZER 1969, 174–198; WEBER 1971; ROLLEY et al. 1983; MORGAN 1990, 43–47; ROLLEY 1992; DE POLIGNAC 1996; KIDERLEN 2010.

[40] Most recently KYRIELEIS 2011, 58–61. For the numbers see KIDERLEN 2010, 96.

[41] ULF 1997b, 41–43 states briefly the problematic character of the first two questions and suggests common feasts with a variety of social activities and interregional communication as an answer for the third.

All these questions, but especially the last one, seem to be extremely hard to answer with some confidence and accuracy today,[42] and in some recent publications they have not even been formulated.[43] Up to a few decades ago, however, there was an easy and seemingly convincing explanation, which connected these offerings with the well-known athletic contests and interpreted them as prizes or victory monuments in the early Olympic Games.[44] Although this view is rightly abandoned today, no really convincing explanation has been put forward instead.

One question of fundamental importance concerning the function or usage of these vessels should be discussed at the outset, although it is usually neglected or treated in a cursory way. It is often assumed that the tripod cauldrons were merely votive objects meant for display and cannot have been used for any practical purpose.[45] This assumption is backed simply by referring to the huge size of some of them, but it is quite misleading in my opinion. Even if it were true for the largest pieces, it would not mean that it can be generalized for the majority with significantly smaller dimensions.[46] In fact, tripod cauldrons were

---

[42] See e.g. LEE 1988, 116 note 10: „It is not necessary that all the tripods have something to do with athletics; some may and some may not."

[43] KIDERLEN 2010; KYRIELEIS 2011.

[44] For a summary see SINN 1991, 31–38.

[45] WEBER 1971; MAASS 1978, 65; 1981, 7; LANGDON 1987, 108.

[46] There are only a few fragments reaching a colossal format (up to 3 m high: MAASS 1978, 73 note 45: Nos. 221, 223, 240) the „normal" pieces being even in this latest group significantly smaller (MAASS 1978, 75), between ca. 1.5–2 m at maximum. The largest Gratbein-Dreifuss (MAASS 1978, No. 176) had feets of ca. 1.7 m high, and earlier variants did not exceed ca. 1 m. (MAASS 1978, 23, 49) Moreover, MAASS 1978, 66–67 clearly describes the results of an experimental reconstruction, which proved beyond doubt that even the largest pieces constructed of sheet bronze are remarkably strong, i.e. can support several hundreds of kilograms. This feature strongly argues for a practical usage and does not support the idea that the largest pieces were meant just for display. The fact that there are no extant bases for tripod cauldrons in Olympia (MAASS 1978, 52) and that at least one of the pieces discovered at Ithaka had wheels (BENTON 1935, 65, Fig. 15) may also suggest that they were regularly moved, i.e. used and not exhibited permanently as statues. The height of the largest tripod legs was considered as a decisive argument against their practical usage (the heat of an ordinary fire could not have effectively reached the cauldron), but considering the practical conditions of their usage, this argument is actually not necessarily valid either. The legs were certainly not just standing on but pierced into the soil, because this was the only means for securing them in their normal position. (This assumption is corroborated by the conspicuous lack of horizontal bars between the legs, which could

originally used as cooking or water-heating vessels,[47] and it is quite reasonable to assume that the dedicated pieces were also used in this way (either before dedication or afterwards or both, most probably only in the sanctuary itself),[48] since there are some clear signs of rubbing, i.e. cleaning them, which can only have become necessary because of their intensive usage over fire.[49] Moreover, eating and drinking in (or in the immediate vicinity of) the sanctuary[50] and the typical animal sacrifices regularly conducted at Olympia make it virtually certain that ritual feasting, involving the roasting and cooking of the meat was actually practised here.[51] Now what makes the cauldrons especially suitable for the purpose of cooking (apart from their legs and open form) is their vertical handles attached to their rim: a staff or rod driven through them could be easily used to lift them while they were still hot and filled with stew.[52] All the subsequent kinds of cauldrons retain these handles, the difference being only that they are not fixed in their vertical position but hinged. Their functionality is not reduced by this change but is perhaps improved, the joint being more robust. The practical usage of the vessels is thus explained: They essentially belonged to the equipment used for ritual dining or feasting in the sanctuary. This is perfectly in accordance with the few archaic inscriptions on similar vessels, and the objects carrying them have correctly been interpreted as cult utensils.[53] It remains to be discussed, whether

---

have been employed to stabilize the tripod, but would have prevented pushing the legs into the soil.) Now as time passed, the ash remains from earlier sacrifices must have accumulated on the site, and because these layers were of relatively loose structure, they necessitated longer tripod legs. They were thus presumably sunk deep into the ash and the soil and the cauldrons were accordingly not placed so high as it would seem from the dimensions of the legs. So heating them by fire presented no difficulties and they could have been used for cooking as well.

[47] SCHWENDEMANN 1921, 120, 144; COLDSTREAM 2003, 317–318; MAASS 1981, 6.
[48] BURKERT 1972, 116; 1988, 33–34; SANSONE 1988, 88–91. That the practice of cooking remained and was of primary importance is clearly attested by Her. 1.59.
[49] Personal communication by M. Kiderlen (Berlin), who conducts a project involving scientific analyses on Greek geometric tripods.
[50] MALLWITZ 1988 (pits for drinking water); KYRIELEIS 2011, 77–79 (spits for roasting; BAITINGER – VÖLLING 2007, 66–87 list 129 examples and state that far more were discovered. It is beyond doubt that they were used for roasting).
[51] As BURKERT 1977, 108–119 clearly showed, the myth of Pelops, with his dismemberment and cooking is also obviously connected with this practice. Cf. also the discussion in the last chapter.
[52] BENTON 1935, 94.
[53] SIEWERT 1991.

the ritual feast was celebrated during the Panhellenic festival and the dedication was thus connected with the *agon* or was independent from the athletic and equestrian events and should be placed in another context.

In order to approach this question, one has to focus first on the dedicators. As the style of the cauldrons suggests, they were not manufactured by local craftsmen, at least most of them are likely to have come from a considerable distance, and the same can be supposed to apply for the dedicators as well. Of course, some local dedicators cannot be ruled out definitely,[54] but simply the exceptionally large number of the pieces and their material value strongly argue against assuming that the majority would have been commissioned and dedicated by local people. The wealthy commissioners could have belonged to the local elite attracting highly expensive products or specialized manufacturers from distant regions and could in theory have dedicated the cauldrons on their own, but during the later centuries, when the evidence is more abundant, there are no signs of such a practice. Costly dedications made by local people in the archaic period are not recorded by Pausanias and were not unearthed by the excavators, whereas evidence for dedicators as well artists from abroad is abundant.[55] This accords well with the general impression that the site was a neutral place far from the important political centres, and was frequented by many different people partly for this reason.[56]

The question if the tripod cauldrons were dedicated by rich individuals or by entire communities cannot be decided. The surviving inscriptions on later vessels with a similar function mention both, even if communities are more numerous.[57] Anyway, whole communities (apart from those in the immediate vicinity) could not come to visit and to offer their votives but had to be represented by a few and certainly rich individuals. Wealthy individuals on the other hand were only able to make such expensive offerings, even if they dedicated them on their own, by exploiting the resources of their subordinate communities – so this question is not especially relevant in my opinion.[58] What is more important, I think, is that the dedicators came from a wide geographical area and that they competed

---

[54] This view is defended by KIDERLEN 2010.

[55] See the representative sample given by Pausanias 5. 21–25.

[56] MORGAN 1990, 45; ULF 1997b, 43.

[57] GAUER 1991, 179 Le 12 (Br 718: spartiatai); 181 Le 26 (B 8347: waleioi); 184 Le 38 (B 458: waleioi); Le 39 (B 4639: waleioi); 186 Le 53 (B 10539: athenaios).

[58] ULF 1997b, 41–42 insists on the communal character of these votives and seems not to realize this point.

with each other in style, workmanship, size, and perhaps even in the number of their offerings. This phenomenon has been aptly described as a „peer-polity interaction".[59]

The occasion for dedicating the tripod cauldrons is far more difficult to determine. Given the absence of explicit contemporary literary testimonia or inscriptions, one can mainly rely on the objects themselves and on later parallels to construct their ritual background. This was the method used earlier as well: thus, because archaic vase-paintings show athletes with tripods behind them and because on a relief decorating a tripod-leg two men fight over a tripod, the dedications were connected with the athletic contests and it was assumed that the victors received them as prizes and dedicated them afterwards to the god.[60] As a corroboration, the athletic events held by Achilles at the funeral games of Patroklos (Hom. *Il.* 23. 257–897)[61] were cited, where the winners also received similar gifts.

However, the single depiction of an athletic contest was plausibly interpreted as a representation of a mythical event,[62] and the chronology of the tripods seems to suggest an earlier inception of the dedications than the traditional date of the first Olympic Games. This latter argument is of course not absolutely decisive on its own, since the beginning of the games cannot be fixed with absolute accuracy, i.e. there might have been earlier athletic events,[63] but the discrepancy remains and raises doubts. Even if there were earlier games than recorded by the victor list, they are not likely to have attracted many participants from distant regions from the very beginning, so they can hardly be connected with the tripod cauldrons. The exceptionally large number of tripods is an equally serious objection, though perhaps not decisive either.[64] As for the Homeric parallel, it would be relevant only if the Olympic Games would represent a similar funeral ceremony, as is the case of Patroklos. In fact, it is assumed that the games had such an origin,

---

[59] SNODGRASS 1986, 54.
[60] SCHWEITZER 1969, 174, HERRMANN 1972, 77; SANSONE 1988, 89.
[61] GARDINER 1930, 20–26; DECKER 1995, 27–34.
[62] MAASS 1978, 56.
[63] As suggested by some ancient sources (listed by the introduction to the Eusebian list of stadion victors ll. 38–45, CHRISTESEN 2007, 153–157, 387) and modern researchers as well (e.g. by HERRMANN 1972, 78–79).
[64] One can e.g. assume more athletic events at the early Olympic games than those implied by the traditional victor list, or games which were held more frequently, e.g. every year, or that every participant received some kind of award, as it was the case at the funeral games of Patroklos.

but this theory is far from certain,[65] and from later centuries it is clear that at Olympia there were no prizes, apart from the wild olive crown, so one can hardly imagine a local organizing committee commissioning tripods and then giving them to the winners (or participants) at the earlier stages of the games.[66] But even if this had been the case, the problem still remains, how and why these cauldrons finally ended up in the sanctuary, because there is only one single possibility which can be envisaged to connect them with the games, i.e. that the cauldrons were dedicated by the victors after their victory, like bronze statues in later periods. However, this practice is not attested by the Homeric poems, and the dedication of tripod cauldrons after athletic victories is not even documented in later periods, although they were used as symbols of victory e.g. in military and dramatic contexts. Moreover, the Homeric poems mention athletic and equestrian games even in the immediate vicinity of Olympia (Hom. *Il.* 23. 626–650)[67] but obviously do not mention the Olympic Games. This can hardly be reconciled with the material evidence, if we take the cauldrons to be connected with the games, since they are most abundant exactly in the period when the poems are supposed to have taken shape, i.e. at the end of the 8th and beginning of the 7th century. From Homer we should thus infer that the Olympic Games were still a relatively unimportant local phenomenon, whereas the cauldrons imply, on the other hand, that the games boomed and were frequented by a large, almost Panhellenic public.[68] This is hardly possible and can be avoided simply by abandoning the notion of the cauldrons somehow arising from the athletic events.[69]

---

[65] ULF – WEILER 1980.

[66] Rightly pointed out by HERRMANN 1972, 77–78.

[67] Hom. *Il.* 11. 699–704 mentions equestrian games organized by Augeias in Elis, which could be tentatively identified with the Olympic Games, but the passage is suspected to be a late addition, since four-horse chariots are not known in the epos. GARDINER 1930, 21.

[68] Already observed by SINN 1991, 34.

[69] LEE 1988, 112 suggests instead that we accept the victor list as a sign of the relatively unimportant character of the games (an assumption not quite sound for several reasons) and that we connect this with the silence of Homer. This line of reasoning makes a strange distinction between sanctuary cult and athletic events, although it assumes quite correctly that the latter were intimately connected with the cult and gives no explanation for the archaeological reality, which clearly shows the supraregional popularity of the sanctuary. The question thus remains why the sanctuary was so famous (if not for the athletic events) and why the athletic events were so unimportant, while the sanctuary became more and more popular and why this situation changed later in the archaic period.

It can be readily discerned on the other hand that not every victor erected or received a monument even in later centuries. Indeed, even famous or multiple victors of the early archaic age (Koroibos, Oibotas, Orsippos, Arrichion),[70] who were remembered several centuries later (and therefore must have been well-known to their contemporaries as well) were not celebrated in this way, and there is no hint that they would have erected tripods for their victories. Most statues were in fact only erected in the classical period or even later,[71] so it is quite reasonable to assume that expensive dedications following an athletic victory were not the general rule from the geometric period but began sporadically during the archaic age and increased only afterwards.

Finally, the supposed dedication of cauldrons after athletic victories cannot explain the subsequent history of similar dedications, i.e. of oriental cauldrons and similar vessels of the archaic age. While the popularity and the number of events i.e. the number of victors increased from the 7th century, the number of cauldrons seems to have decreased during this period.[72] One may therefore assume a change in the frequency of the games (from annual to the traditional penteteric periodicity), or some kind of economic crisis during the 7th century effecting a change in the practice of erecting victory monuments. The first change (to be discussed below) would itself call for an explanation, which is not easy given the rising popularity of the athletic events, for the second there is no real support in the remaining votive material, which shows no signs of impoverishment but rather increasing wealth. So neither hypothesis can adequately explain the anomaly. Moreover, the disappearance of the large tripod cauldrons does not mean that other vessels with a similar function would have disappeared during the archaic age. The orientalizing cauldrons most obviously follow this tradition

---

[70] MORETTI 1957, nos. 6, 16, 42–43, 102.

[71] HERRMANN 1988, 123–125 giving the exact numbers for different periods according to Pausanias and the actual finds respectively. Notwithstanding the unknown reasons for the divergences, the data show the same evolution from the archaic to the classical period.

[72] The original number of cauldrons in different periods can of course not be determined exactly, but a rough estimate can be made, since it is most probably not by chance that there are (according to the publications given in note 38) clearly more than 300 fragments of tripod cauldrons representing ca. 200–300 pieces according to MAASS 1978, 2, but significantly less than 200 protomes and oriental(izing) attachments, implying a considerably lower total number of dedications.

and the exceptionally large number of bronze handles and revetments[73] strongly suggest that the dedicatory practice remained in later centuries as well, and that it was only the style and the size of the vessels that changed but not their practical function.

The early appearance, high numbers, and wide geographical distribution of the cauldrons can thus not be explained by the Panhellenic *agon* and it is appropriate to consider alternative hypotheses offered instead of interpreting them as athletic victory monuments.

In a general discussion of bronze votives dedicated in geometric sanctuaries, the cauldrons were interpreted – along with the contemporary bronze figurines – as gifts offered by aristocrats to the gods in return for or assuring their own status, legitimacy and other claims in a similar way, as contemporary individuals exchanged gifts for similar immaterial benefits.[74] This explanation is not entirely convincing, since it does not differentiate between the various kinds of dedications, which are indeed of rather different size, value and significance and cannot account for (and does not even attempt to consider) the regional differences or peculiar distribution patterns, such as the concentration of certain votive types in Olympia.[75] So this theory cannot solve the problem of the cauldron dedications at Olympia. There are, however, two other distinct and unrelated but not necessarily contradictory types of reasoning, developed parallel to each other, which concern more specifically Olympia and its tripod cauldrons. C. Morgan, who primarily addressed the problem from an economic and social perspective and explicitly argued against their connection with the games, interpreted the tripods as a form of conspicuous consumption practised by the elites of distant regions.[76] She did not consider the religious aspects of the dedication, i.e. the deity honoured and did not try to define the occasions more closely.[77] U. Sinn, however was the

---

[73] GAUER 1991, 178–235 lists more than 500 fragments belonging to different kinds of cauldrons.

[74] LANGDON 1987.

[75] The distribution pattern has been considered in detail by POLIGNAC 1996, but regarding the great sanctuaries the results he reached are remarkably similar to those of Langdon (whose work is not mentioned by him).

[76] MORGAN 1990, 43–47. In a similar way, HIMMELMANN 2002, 93 interprets the tripods just like valuable objects, premonetary symbols of wealth dedicated as dekate for the god. However, after the invention of money, it was not customary to dedicate coins, so this interpretation is similarly beyond proof, as the others, criticised by Himmelmann.

[77] She has been followed by ULF 1997b, 37–39, but was criticised for this by HERRMANN 1991.

first to elaborate another theory which aimed precisely at this point. Based on an otherwise neglected passage in Strabo (8. 3.30 C 353), he argued that the sanctuary was primarily not famous for its games, but for the oracle of Zeus, which was mainly concerned with military affairs and attracted many Greeks from the western colonies, who felt indebted to the oracle.[78] The argument is backed by the large amount of archaic arms and armour dedicated in the sanctuary and is perfectly sound for interpreting them,[79] but the military oracle does not explain the dedication pattern of the geometric tripod cauldrons. Perhaps it is exactly for this reason that in most of his publications Sinn does not explicitly mention them, and the connection of tripods with the oracle occurs only in his shortest general introduction to Olympia and its games.[80] J. Taita, who accepts this theory in general, implies a connection between the tripod cauldrons and the warlike oracle, but does not state this explicitly.[81] Indeed, there is a much wider chronological gap between the first attested appearance of the oracle[82] and the appearance of the tripods than between the first games and the tripods. Admittedly, tripods were occasionally used as monuments in later times at Olympia and Delphi for commemorating military victories[83] (unlike athletic ones), but it would be strange to assume so many military conflicts of great importance in this early period. At any rate, the dedicatory inscriptions found on the vessels in Olympia do not support this idea, since they never hint at military victories (unlike those on the weapons). One also wonders, how the oracle became so well-known to a wide public at an early date, but was completely neglected already in the archaic age

---

[78] SINN 1991, 38–49; 1996, 22–29; 2004, 58–60; 2010, 82–83.
[79] BAITINGER 2011, 76–87.
[80] SINN 1991, 34 mentions the cauldrons just in the introductory overview but not in connection with oracle. The explicit statement is found only in SINN 1996, 27–28.
[81] TAITA 2009, 381–382.
[82] Schol. Pind. Ol. 6.6 (referring to the participation of Agesias, an Olympic seer in the foundation of Syrakousai). It is far from certain that Pindar intended the line, as it is interpreted by the scholion (and accepted by WENIGER 1915, 68–72 and KETT 1966, 18–20), i.e. that it was an ancestor of Agesias who assisted the first colonists in the 8th century. Another equally (or rather more) plausible interpretation is to take the statement literally and to assume that Agesias was somehow involved in the recent enlargement of the city by Gelon. This view is succinctly stated by WILAMOWITZ 1922, 307.
[83] Olympia: Paus. 5.10.4 (acroteria of the temple of Zeus), Delphi: Paus. 10.13.9 (dedication after Plataea), Diod. 11.26.7 (Deinomenid dedications).

by Croesus.[84] The connection between the basic function of the cauldrons and the oracle is also unexplained, since this type of vessel was not directly involved in the divinatory practice at Olympia (unlike at Dodona or Delphi). Judging by the number of the preserved fragments of tripod cauldrons, one would assume that the oracle at Olympia had attained a greater and earlier fame than Delphi,[85] but according to the literary sources Apollo Pythios was clearly more important in this respect and it was even regarded as the source of the Olympian oracle.[86] So this institution, however important it was, cannot be used to explain the early appearance nor the wide geographical origin of the tripods, and one has to look out for other possibilities.

As the practice of dedicating tripod cauldrons is clearly connected with ritual feasting and predates in all probability both the athletic contests and the military oracle one should look for an explanation which is both early or rather primitive and can serve at the same time as a common source for both characteristic features of the sanctuary. On the other hand, it should explain why the élites of distant regions and their dedications were attracted to the sanctuary to an unparalleled extent.

The clue is likely to be found by analysing the other most distinctive class of votive objects, the animal figurines. They were, contrary to the tripods, never connected with the Olympic Games, were indeed treated as an isolated group of dedications, clearly attesting that the sanctuary had nothing to do with athletic contests during the Early Iron Age. As the discussion will show, they clearly deserve a closer scrutiny and can reveal the real origins of the Games.

Animal Figurines

At Olympia the earliest dedications were small votive figurines made of clay and bronze. Several thousands have been discovered in the „Black stratum", and one can hardly guess how many were actually dedicated. It is appropriate, I think, to deal primarily with the metal dedications, because they are far more numerous and thus lend themselves better to statistical analysis, and because their interpretation is crucial for the understanding of the early history of the sanctuary. On the basis of previous studies, it seems to be safe to conclude that these figurines were produced during the 9–8th centuries either by distant workshops in Argos, Korinth

---

[84] Her. 1.46–49.
[85] MAASS 1992, 85; 1993, 127 (with previous literature).
[86] Pind. Ol. 6; Her. 9.33.

and Lakonia or by itinerant bronzesmiths coming from these regions and working temporarily at Olympia.[87]

The exceptionally large number and the widely scattered origin of the bronze animal figurines are remarkable and require some special explanation. However, the reasons for their dedication have been sought in vain so far and the phenomenon has received only cursory treatment.[88] What the figurines actually depict seemed so obvious that it has never been properly discussed: they were identified as domesticated animals, and the figurines were generally supposed to have been dedicated by the owners / herdsmen for the prosperity / fertility of

---

[87] The abundant literature (e.g. FURTWÄNGLER 1890, HEILMEYER 1979, HERRMANN 1964, ZIMMERMANN 1989) is summarized and thoroughly discussed by ANDREWS 1994, 34–150. On-site production is absolutely clear, and it is generally assumed that the craftsmen working here were most probably itinerant (cf. note 92 below). A certain (and not insignificant) proportion of the figurines is usually considered as the product of „local" craftsmen, imitating imported prototypes or emulating their visiting fellows. HEILMEYER 1979, 275 counted 4042 animals and considers (*ibid.* 137) 568 pieces as products of foreign workshops, but admits that the entire „local" production was more or less dependent on the Argive school. „Local" style defined in this way could be simply termed as provincial Argive and is not necessarily more local than the one constituting the Argive school proper, which is also mainly known (especially in its earliest phase) from pieces found at Olympia. Defining 'local' by extending the meaning of the term to embrace both Messenia and Arkadia, as done by MORGAN 1990, is problematic as well, for precisely those regions which lie closest to Olympia do not show any marked connections with the sanctuary. ZIMMERMANN 1989, 63 argues for a much higher percentage of foreign imports (43–47% of the horses) than Heilmeyer and shows that the stylistic judgments on which these estimates are based are bound to be highly subjective, and the matter cannot be settled with absolute certainty. It is, however, highly improbable that bronzesmiths working permanently in this region specialised exclusively in small figurine dedications and since other local bronze products (e.g. tripods, weapons, etc.) and indeed major settlements or cemeteries are entirely missing, it is not very likely that most of the figurines were produced by local craftsmen, however we define the meaning of this term.

[88] For the animal figurines in general: HEILMEYER 1979, 195–197; PILALI 1986, 160; SINN 2010, 81. BEVAN 1986, 89 (bovines), 204–206 (horses). The following conclusion (PRENT 2005, 394) concerns similar dedications made at Cretan sanctuaries, but is entirely fitting for Olympia as well: „This popularity … makes it difficult to give universal explanations which go beyond 'substitute for sacrificial animal' or 'something pleasing to the deity'. … in some cases the offering of a bronze animal figurine may reflect the wealth in livestock of the dedicator."

their animals or for some other reasons.⁸⁹ This general view (which has already been severely criticized by Herrmann⁹⁰) is challenged here and a new hypothesis is put forward, suggesting a different interpretation and context for the geometric votive offerings at Olympia, which may help in explaining the origins of the Panhellenic character of the sanctuary and its games as well.

Some singular pieces and the human figures apart, the bronze figurines represent two kinds of animals: horses and cattle.⁹¹ The horses have been studied more thoroughly and mainly from an art historical point of view. Their rendering is not uniform, but displays characteristic features attested in different regions of the Peloponnese, and can thus be used to identify the manufacturers' place of origin.⁹² The bulls or bovines are equally various, but have fewer parallels elsewhere. The most numerous group, which is most similar to the material from Olympia both in general appearance and in terms of chronology, comes from

---

⁸⁹ HEILMEYER 1972, 87–88; SINN 1981, 37–38; MORGAN 1993, 22; SCHÜRMANN 1996, 219–220; TAITA 2009, 378–379. Other kinds of votive offerings depicting animals were treated in a similar manner: GUGGISBERG 1996, 335–341; BAUMBACH 2004, 96, 161–162.

⁹⁰ HERRMANN 1980, 69 n. 67. This criticism has largely gone unnoticed, as far as I can see.

⁹¹ HEILMEYER 1979, 196 gives the following statistics concerning the animal figurines: „53,84% Rinder, 45,21% Pferde". In absolute numbers (ibid. 275): 1885 cattle and 1583 horses out of a total of 4042. In other sanctuaries, e.g. Delphi, Athenian Acropolis, Argive Heraion, the horse figurines are usually more numerous than the bovids, which might be totally or nearly absent in the geometric period (e.g. at Kalapodi and Philia).

⁹² HERRMANN 1964 (cf. HERRMANN 1972, 232 n. 265). ZIMMERMANN 1989 arrives at significantly different results, but the approach of Herrmann remains more convincing and seems to be generally accepted (HEILMEYER 1979; ROLLEY 1994, 97–101; COLDSTREAM 2003). BOL 2002, 7–8 argues however that the assumption of local styles raises fundamental problems and is not corroborated by the available evidence. He assumes that the majority of the votives were produced on site and denies the possibility of determining the origins of the craftsmen, who were in his view not itinerant foreigners but permanently settled local ones. A thorough discussion of this proposition is perhaps inappropriate here, but it should be stressed that Bol's theory does not offer any specific explanation for the peculiar distribution pattern of the figurines, i.e. for their abundance in Olympia and for their low numbers elsewhere, nor can it account for the rapid decline of the presumably local production. Moreover, Bol does not consider questions of the metal supply (discussed at length by ANDREWS 1994) or the relation between sacred and profane economy (cf. MORGAN 2003), all of which would, in my opinion, argue against his view. The assumption of local schools of geometric metalworkers still seems to be valid.

Crete.⁹³ In other sanctuaries and regions there are just sporadic pieces or, in the case of the Kabeirion, mainly later series.⁹⁴ In fact the geometric bull figurines from Olympia account for ca. 75–80% of all the comparable contemporary material.⁹⁵ The percentage is quite similar in the case of horse figurines,⁹⁶ the

---

⁹³ PILALI 1985 enumerating 172 pieces, most of them from Hagia Triada, Phaistos and Psychro. SCHÜRMANN 1996 lists 325 geometric bull figurines from a single sanctuary, Kato Syme Viannou.

⁹⁴ Apart from the pieces which were found at Olympia, Crete and the Kabeirion and are discussed here, geometric bronze cattle figurines are in fact extremely rare (noted e.g. by LANGDON 1987, 62; cf. HEILMEYER 1979, 194–195 listing sporadic examples from the vicinity of Olympia and SCHMALTZ 1980, 140 enumerating the pieces known at that time from major and minor sanctuaries all over Greece; a more complete list is compiled in Appendix II). BEVAN 1986, 378–389 lists representations of cattle in various materials and ranging from the Mycenaean to the Classical period, but recognized the strange distribution pattern as well. Bronze bull figurines of later periods (found e.g. at Athens, Delphi, Perachora, Argive Heraion) and those made of other materials, such as terracotta or lead, are not significantly more numerous either (SCHMALTZ 1980, 141), especially if compared to the geometric material found at Olympia.

⁹⁵ The chronology of the pieces from the Kabeirion is controversial and affects the estimate significantly. SCHMALTZ 1980 assigned 126 bulls to the geometric period, but this result was contested with good reasons by LANGDON 1982, 596, who argued convincingly, in my view, for a much lower figure: „Certain of his (i.e. Schmaltz's) figures may indeed be Geometric (nos. 100–106), but I see no reason to place any of the steers before the late 8ᵗʰ c., and would suggest that most are archaic." The sporadic pieces listed in Appendix II and the geometric material from the Kabeirion are thus estimated at ca. 50–100 pieces, the Cretan material (cf. above note 93) at ca. 500. Concerning Olympia, the figure given by HEILMEYER 1979, 275 ("1885 Rinder") seems to be more reliable than the other, much lower one by ZIMMERMANN 1989, 63 n. 2 ("1323 bovidés"). cf. note 96 below. ZIMMERMANN 1989, 2 states that Olympia and the Kabeirion share 95% of all known examples from the geometric period, but gives no exact figures and seems not to have taken into account the material from Crete (which was known at least partially for him by PILALI 1985) or did not calculate, but simply expressed an impression. (Any calculation starting from his 1323 pieces for Olympia and taking into account the 172 pieces reported by PILALI 1985 gives max. 89%.) Thus the entire material is estimated at ca. 2500 pieces and the overall share of Olympia seems to reach ca. 75–77%, Crete ca. 20%, the rest, including the Kabeirion about ca. 3–5%.

⁹⁶ The percentage of the geometric horse figurines found in Olympia compared to the corpus of ca. 1200 Greek geometric pieces assembled by ZIMMERMANN 1989, is given (ibidem p. 63) as 82 %. This figure is based on Zimmermann's own count of the figurines at Olympia (ibidem n.2: "979 équidés"), which is markedly different from the

main difference being that the remaining material is not uniformly scattered but concentrated almost exclusively on Crete. In this region the representation and religious significance of the animal had a well-known and long-established tradition,[97] but Bronze Age traditions cannot account for the appearance of the numerous bronze bulls, and it seems to be significant that some general similarities

Fig. 1. Bronze bovine figurines found at Kato Syme (Crete)
© Deutsches Archäologisches Institut, Athen

---

figure given by HEILMEYER 1979, 275 ("1583 Pferde"). The arithmetical inaccuracies of ZIMMERMANN 1989 were rightly pointed out by Heilmeyer in his review (Gnomon 63, 1991, 658), but apart from the difference concerning the number of pieces found at Olympia, Zimmermann's corpus can be safely taken as representative regarding the numbers of Greek geometric horse figurines. Starting from this assumption, one can estimate that roughly 210–250 pieces are known from outside Olympia and by comparing this figure with the one given by Heilmeyer for the horses of Olympia, the sanctuary's share would rise only to around 87 %, which is not significantly higher than the figure given by Zimmermann.

[97] For details see von LENGERKEN 1955, 121–145; PILALI 1985, 124–127; MCINERNEY 2010, 48–73.

apart, the Cretan bulls (*Fig. 1*) are technically and stylistically quite different from those found on the Greek mainland, and were associated with different kinds of votive figurines (mainly rams and goats, instead of horses, which occur only sporadically on Crete) than at Olympia.[98] On Crete the manufacturers and the dedicators clearly come from the neighbouring region, i.e. central Crete, while at Olympia, the producers and/or the votives originate, at least in part, from distant regions.

What do we know about the dedicators? Although the figurines at Olympia are more various in their place of origin than their Cretan counterparts, the earliest dedicators at Olympia are equally supposed to be local ones. The implications of such a hypothesis have not been recognized, so they deserve to be mentioned here.

Assuming such a scenario, it would be first unexplained, in comparison to the Cretan case, why local people around Olympia would and could have attracted bronzesmiths or their products from distant regions. It is obviously possible to assume that local people around Olympia were more prosperous than those on Crete and could afford elaborate dedications in much greater quantities, since Elis was renowned for its agrarian wealth from the late classical period. Mythology also located large herds of cattle in this region,[99] but clearly identifiable dedications made by individuals from Elis (attested e.g. by dedicatory inscriptions) are practically unknown at Olympia at any time (most important in this context is certainly their absence during the archaic age) and large quantities of dedications offered by individual inhabitants of the neighbourhood are therefore not very likely at such an early period either.[100]

---

[98] For stylistic comparisons see PILALI 1985, 177–182; for the technical, stylistic and iconographic idiosyncrasies of the Cretan bronze figurines SCHÜRMANN 1996, 195–214.

[99] Xen. *Hell*. 3.2.26; Polyb. 4.73. For the herds of Augeias see e.g. Paus. 5.1.9. For large herds of exceptional size Livy 27.32.9. The numerical data regarding the size of the herds in this region, which are given by Homer (*Il*. 11. 670–761), are more probably not to be taken literally.

[100] The absence of individual votive inscriptions is of course an argumentum *e silentio*, but it is perhaps more relevant than other similar arguments, since there are some collective dedications made by the Eleans and other local peoples which are attested by inscriptions on a few metal vessels (SIEWERT 1991), so the absence of personal dedications cannot be attributed to a general lack of interest in inscribing votives. To suppose, on the other hand, that the votive figurines would be collective votives, would be quite strange, since there are absolutely no parallels for such a dedicatory praxis.

On the other hand, it is not apparent, assuming local dedicators and considering the parallel case of the Kabeirion, why the dedications would have been made, both on Crete and in Olympia, only during the geometric period and why the supposed dedicators ceased to continue this practice in later centuries. General trends can be invoked for this change,[101] but as the large quantities seem to be a local speciality at both places, and since they seem to be unrelated, one would expect an equally local cause for the abandoning of the practice as well.

Supposing external dedicators in Olympia is therefore more likely, even if some problems seem to remain open. For instance, it is not clear why all the wealthy cattle and horse owners (or at least most of them) would have come from the Argolid, Korinth and Lakonia equally and precisely to Olympia, and why they offered such simple and inexpensive votive dedications and only during the geometric period. An answer to the first question referring to the fame of the sanctuary, is absolutely unconvincing for this early period, characterised as it was by isolated settlement nuclei and restricted communications.[102] As attested by the large and expensive tripod dedications, the fame of the sanctuary was clearly emerging in this period, but this reputation should not be taken for granted from the earliest periods and it should be rather explained than used to explain contemporary phenomena. As a source for the sanctuary's reputation, the ancient sources offer two explanations: the Olympic Games and the oracle of Zeus.[103] Neither can be safely dated back to the geometric period and the bronze figurines have apparently nothing to do with either. An ancient (fertility) cult of a female goddess was proposed by modern commentators partly on the basis of late literary testimonia and partly because of the numerous animal figurines,[104] but even if this hypothesis were essentially correct, it can hardly explain on its own the wide and rather peculiar spread of the cult. For it is beyond reasonable doubt that external dedicators are not likely to have come from the vicinity, particularly from

---

[101] SNODGRASS 1989/1990 developed the idea of a change from „raw" to „converted" dedications and interpreted the bronze animal figurines in this context (ibid. p. 292) as „raw" ones „dedicated on the occasion of a sacrifice of an animal" and disappearing at the beginning of the classical period, along with other kinds of „raw" dedications.
[102] ULF 1997b, 37–40.
[103] Strab. 8.3.30.
[104] HERRMANN 1962; SINN 2010, 81; ROBERTSON 2010, 70–73.

Messenia, Arcadia or Achaia, but from more remote areas.[105] This observation strongly militates against the theory of a simple fertility cult spreading gradually.

It is thus worth considering in detail who the dedicators might have been and why the small figurines were offered in the sanctuary. As the figurines were relatively easy to produce and therefore cheap, and because they are present in large quantities, one is tempted to suppose a large number of relatively poor dedicators and mainly local ones. But none of these reasons is compelling: low costs imply poor dedicators only if we assume that each dedicator left just one figurine (or a few) and nothing else in the sanctuary, and this is by no means certain (all might have dedicated dozens or even hundreds of figurines at a single occasion and also other objects as well); the large numbers are likely to result from the large number of visitors, but may be also explained by recurring visits by the same, relatively small group of visitors, who may come from any distance. At any rate, the producers of the figurines came mainly from the same areas as those of the large tripod cauldrons and it is therefore reasonable to suppose that the accumulation of small dedications in Olympia is equally due to the exceptionally strong attraction and supraregional importance of the sanctuary, and is not a purely local phenomenon. This consideration actually argues for the assumption that as in the case of the tripods the dedicators of the figurines were of the same origins as their producers, i.e. they were most probably external visitors of the sanctuary, coming mainly from the NE and southern Peloponnese. And if they came from such distant areas, they are likely to have been wealthy enough to afford such a trip. Is it possible that the dedicators of the tripods and those of the figurines were identical? I think it is reasonable to assume that they were,[106] because otherwise (assuming that the number of figurines indicates roughly the number of dedicators or the number of their visits) the numerous figurines would require a high number of relatively wealthy dedicators in addition to those dedicating the tripods, and

---

[105] MORGAN 1993, 22. In theory, it would be possible to suppose dedicators coming neither from the neighbourhood of the sanctuary nor from the home of the votive producers but from anywhere else (e.g. the intermediary regions listed above), but there is no evidence supporting this view.

[106] MORGAN 1993, 24 clearly differentiates the dedicators of the figurines from those of the tripods and supposes two different social groups, connecting the animal figurines to the „average visitor" and the tripods to „the richer man". The horse figurines do not fit this pattern, even according to MORGAN (1993, 23), and there is nothing to prove it in the case of the bovines.

all being able to afford a visit to the distant sanctuary.[107] Numerous well-to-do visitors are not very likely to be found anywhere during the geometric period and are especially unlikely to be present at Olympia before ca. 700 B.C., when the first pits were dug to provide drinking water for a large number of people.[108] That, on the other hand, the two groups of dedications were intimately connected is clearly shown by the bull heads on the earliest cauldron handles and by the numerous horse figurines on the later ones.[109] Moreover, since the large number of cauldrons implies an equally large number of animals to be prepared in them, it would be quite logical to search for a cult context, which could account for dedicating both types of object (i.e. tripod cauldrons and animal figurines) by the same group of dedicators.

In order to settle the question of the dedicators one could possibly consider the material of the figurines as well. The fact that there are significantly fewer pieces made of terracotta than bronze, is however a warning signal not to interpret the material as an indicator of the dedicators' wealth. If clay signified poorer dedicators, one would expect more pieces made of terracotta, especially in the case of local dedicators. So either we take the material as indicating the means of the dedicator and conclude that wealthy dedicators were more numerous than the poor, or we simply disregard the difference in value of the material. In fact, even the metal figurines cannot have been especially expensive, but this does not necessarily mean that the dedicators were poor ones. Wealthy visitors could also offer cheap figurines.

There are in addition two obvious and peculiar facts which call for some kind of explanation. The first is the exceptionally large number of dedicated pieces as compared with both contemporary and later sanctuaries; the other is the assemblage of the material in Olympia, i.e. the relative percentages of the species depicted. As already mentioned, at least ca. 90% of the bronze material is made up of cattle and horses, which are represented continuously (i.e. without much fluctuation over the centuries under discussion) in more or less equal numbers.[110] This ratio is unparalleled elsewhere, as in most cases horses

---

[107] Admittedly, it is possible that one dedicator left a herd of figurines in the sanctuary, and in this way the number of dedicators could decrease dramatically. This possibility will be discussed below, at the end of this section.

[108] MALLWITZ 1988, 1999, 196–199.

[109] MAASS 1978, esp. 18 note 26 with a list of bulls' heads on early tripod handles.

[110] SNODGRASS 1987, 206 fig. 64 would imply a marked decrease in the percentage of bull figurines from protogeometric to Geometric times. Even if the adopted chronology

account for the majority of votive figurines, and when the cattle/bulls are more numerous, as in the case of Crete or the Theban Kabeirion, then the horses are almost entirely missing.[111] Moreover, if we look at the role played by the two animals in Greek cult, we see that while bulls were the most prestigious and ubiquitous animals sacrificed, horses were almost never used for this purpose. So what was the common factor in the equally remarkable numbers of horse and cattle figurines? Is there actually a common factor to be expected? Considering the large numbers involved, the approximately equal proportions are unlikely to be accidental, and because the two groups were produced by similar workshops it is plausible that they were dedicated by the same group of people and at a similar frequency. So even if the reason for their dedication was not exactly the same, it can be safely assumed that it was similar. In this case the large number of the Olympia figurines cannot simply be explained by the ordinary sacrificial customs observed all over Greece, and apparently no one is inclined to assume a direct link with real animal sacrifices even for the bovids at Olympia.[112] In such a case, one would certainly be surprised to find that in later centuries the dedication of bull figurines practically disappeared, while the sacrificial practices remained basically the same. Also in the Kabeirion in Boiotia, where bronze cattle figures are similarly abundant and indeed almost the only species represented throughout several centuries, the analysis of the archaeozoological material has shown that in reality these animals were sacrificed rather seldom in comparison with ovicaprids, which are, however only sporadically represented among the votives.[113] According to the available archaeozoological data, this sacrificial pattern prevailed in most Greek sanctuaries[114] and assuming some kind of correlation with the real sacrifices performed in the sanctuaries the generally low frequency of dedicating bull figurines or statues in Greek sanctuaries can be regarded as normal. But on the other hand this underlines the exceptional

---

made it possible to discern such a change, the absolute numbers of pieces involved differ so drastically from each other that statistical comparison between the two sets of data becomes rather meaningless (18 protogeometric versus 1764 geometric pieces).

[111] From Crete there are 7 bronze horse figurines known, four of them decorating vessels and coming from the Ideaen cave. ZIMMERMANN 1989, 293.

[112] SNODGRASS 1989/1990, 292 is a conspicuous exception when he states that: „many of them, at least when they represent cattle, sheep or pigs, *must have been dedicated on the occasion of a sacrifice of an animal or animals of the species in question.*" (my italics)

[113] SCHMALTZ 1980.

[114] HÄGG 1998; FORSTENPOINTER 2003.

character of the cattle figurines at Olympia and suggests that another kind of explanation is needed for their dedication, just as in the case of the Kabeirion.

Considering the sanctuary of Hermes and Aphrodite at Kato Syme on Crete and the Theban Kabeirion, one can see that the recipient deity was clearly not decisive (the figurines could be dedicated to any divinity, just as the living bovids could be sacrificed for any god or goddess), and as most geometric santuaries did not receive cattle figurines in similar quantities, it is equally clear that chronological factors were not responsible either. A common feature of the cults involved, e.g. fertility or initiation can be perhaps supposed, but some more specific local factor seems more likely.[115] Here the famous passage of the *Iliad* (11.670–761) comes to mind, where Nestor related the mutual conflicts of Elis and Pylos. Herd animals were always the cause of the conflicts, and considering the important role played by monuments celebrating military victories in the later history of the sanctuary, it is tempting to connect the early dedications to similar events as well. One could imagine e.g. that after winning a great number of horses and cattle during a raid, as related by Nestor, the victors would have dedicated some figurines representing the booty or the share of the gods. Such a practice is, however, not indicated by the epic: the gods were regularly honoured with animal sacrifices and not with figurines. The commemoration of animal sacrifices in the form of statuettes is not very likely either,[116] since in later centuries, when similar sacrifices were regularly held, it was by no means usual to erect a monument depicting the sacrificial animal[117] and horses were certainly not sacrificed at all. It could be suggested perhaps that the figurines were not commemorating real sacrifices, but were meant as a cheap replacement by those who were unable

---

[115] SCHMALTZ 1980, 1983 101–103 developed the idea that the main reason for the exceptional popularity of cattle figurines was some cultic reason in connection with the deity worshipped both at the Kabeirion and at Olympia. Schmaltz refers in this context to the cult of Dionyos at Elis, where there is marked evidence to show that Dionysos was worshipped in the form of a bull, but does not want to connect the bull figurines of Olympia with this cult. The cult of Zeus in general can hardly account for the thousands of figurines at Olympia either, since cattle figurines are absent from other sanctuaries of Zeus.

[116] Such a practice was plausibly suggested for the terracotta cattle figurines at the Heraion of Samos, since there it is proven by the osteological remains that cattle were the most frequently dedicated animals. BAUMBACH 2004, 161–162 with references.

[117] The bull of the Korkyreans (Paus. 10.9.3-4) is surely an exception that proves the rule.

to sacrifice a real animal.[118] Supposing such a scenario, the dedicators could be poor locals as well as wealthy foreigners, because it is unlikely that they were able to carry their own sacrificial animals from their distant home. However, this hypothesis cannot account for the rapid growth and decline of the dedicatory pattern and would be absolutely incompatible with the large number of horse figurines. The conclusion seems thus to be unavoidable that the figurines are by no means related to ancient Greek animal sacrifices as they were practiced later in most sanctuaries.

Given the differences in the ritual role of horses and cattle, it was supposed that the dedication of these animal figurines, was simply motivated by the everyday living conditions or personal emotions of the dedicators, who were supposed to be mainly ordinary local peasants. In this respect it is interesting to note that emotions concerning cattle and horses were generally quite different and are therefore not likely to account for the roughly equal numbers of the figurines.[119] If this were decisive, horse figurines should far outnumber cattle, as is the case in most other sanctuaries.

The prevailing opinion thus takes the figurines as a reflection of the living conditions of the dedicators themselves, and suggests that the most valuable animals were in this form put under the protection of the divinity.[120] This hypothesis could perhaps explain the presence and the large number of animal figurines in Olympia, if the underlying notion of a large-scale pastoralism during the geometric period in the surrounding region could be substantiated,[121] but is

---

[118] This could be the reason for dedicating hundreds of terracotta bulls (during the 4th–3rd centuries BC) at a rural shrine of Poseidon at Tsiskiana on Crete, where the animal remains originate entirely from ovicaprids. (NINIOU-KINDELI 2003)

[119] LORENZ 2000, 324–325.

[120] HEILMEYER 1972, 1979, GUGGISBERG 1996, SCHÜRMANN 1996. SNODGRASS 1987 took the bull figurines in contrast to the horses as an explicit indicator of pastoralist dedicators, but admits that the horses can not be connected with farmers. It was only SCHMALTZ 1983 who opposed this line of reasoning, but he also failed to give a more convincing interpretation.

[121] The extent of pastoralism and the assumption of large herds in the vicinity of Olympia can rely exclusively on references taken from Homeric epic, from much later sources and the dedication of figurines themselves. As the studies dealing with the problem in general show, a transhumant large-scale pastoralism is very unlikely under the circumstances of the Dark Ages. CHERRY 1988, 27–29 against SNODGRASS 1987. For the entire debate concerning agro-pastoralism versus transhumance see the excellent summary in HOWE 2008, 13–25 and for the Dark Ages especially ibid. 34–38. Considerations based on ethnographic parallels from Africa, where cattle rearing

clearly less suited to account for the conspicuous gaps in the distribution pattern. One wonders for instance, why in Crete the method would have been applied only to cattle, rams, goats and not to horses, and why most well-to-do farmers/ herders in ancient Greece applied this method practically exclusively to their horses and did not choose this simple option for their cattle even in those areas which show marked environmental similarities with Olympia, i.e. are well-suited or even renowned for cattle rearing and/or are clearly in close contact with this sanctuary. The most conspicuous instance belonging to both categories is the case of the Argolid, where the Heraion attracted only horse dedications, but Thessaly is a prime example of the first and Lakonia of the second. So this kind of interpretation should for several reasons not be taken as the definitive explanation for the dedication of animal figurines.

The most important common feature of cattle and horses in ancient Greece was that they were valuable belongings (horses in particular can be termed „luxury items" or „prestige goods") and their relatively cheap representations could therefore be seen as expressing notions connected with wealth and status. If they were dedicated by people wealthy enough to own and to use these animals, they could express their success and pride but also their anxiety about or concerning them; if on the contrary they were dedicated by those who were simply eager to aquire them, the figurines could stand for their hopes. Assuming this last possibility one can hardly see why the practice of dedicating these figurines (especially those of the bovids) did not develop at other places and why the practice disappeared at Olympia as well as at other sanctuaries, since poor people desiring to become more prosperous were certainly present everywhere and in all stages of history and both horses and bovids continued to represent wealth and status during the following centuries as well.[122] So the alternative is to be preferred, because assuming wealthy dedicators one can more easily imagine that they changed their dedicatory fashions for a variety of reasons (e.g. simply because new modes and types of representing their wealth and status emerged). The material from the sanctuary at Kato Syme can be regarded as a nice parallel in this respect. Here the bovine figurines disappeared and were replaced by representations of

---

forms the real basis of the economy and clearly plays an important role in those societies (MCINERNEY 2010) cannot prove that the imaginary world of Homeric epic faithfully depicts the reality during the Dark Ages. While the references to large herds are unlikely to be entirely fanciful, they might derive e.g. from wild or feral animals living in this region, a possibility which will be explored in detail below.

[122] Most recently HOWE 2008, 31–33 and 39–44.

the dedicators themselves, who are characterized as aristocratic hunters engaging in homoerotic affairs, the famous practice of male initiation described by later sources in detail. Further implications of this change will be considered below; in the present context, however, it is important to note that the dedicators were not ordinary or poor local people, but the wealthiest of the surrounding region. The same is most probably true for Olympia as well. For the question of whether the well-to-do „aristocratic" visitors at Olympia were local or mainly external, we have a valuable source of information, namely the victors of the hippic agons. The available data clearly show that these victors always came from outside the surrounding region[123] suggesting therefore that the wealthy owners of the horses, i.e. the presumable descendants of the dedicators of the horse figurines, were (like their manufacturers) also of foreign origin. Of course local aristocrats cannot be excluded altogether, but they are not likely to account for a large percentage of the dedications.

The sheer quantity of the horse figurines points in the same direction as well. From the near contemporary literary sources, i.e. Homer and Hesiod, it is evident that horses were exclusively used for pulling the chariots of the aristocratic warriors and played no role in agricultural activities on a subsistence level.[124] Horses (whether few or many) in the possession of ordinary farmers or herdsmen can therefore be practically excluded and it is appropriate to assume that horse figurines were connected with and dedicated by wealthy people, who can be termed

---

[123] MORETTI 1955 Nos. 33, 52, 81, 96, 103, 106, 110, 113, 117, 120, 124, 127, 136, 141, 147, 151, 152, 157, 164 (listing for the 7–6th centuries victors from Sikyon, Thebes, Athens, Sparta, Epidamnos, Korinthos and Gela) and some more 50 victors from the 5th cent. It is only at the end of this century that local winners appear in hippic contests (MORETTI 1955 Nos. 350, 364, 365). The only local winner in the race of quadrigas is the community of Dyspontion (Moretti No. 39 allegedly at Ol. 27 = 672 BC.) Even if this piece of evidence is historically true, it does not seem to be enough to postulate local winners for the early period, when there is absolutely no information about the winners of the hippic agons. If there were some, or if it could be taken as probable for the contemporaries, Hippias of Elis could have easily introduced even fictive local Elean winners in his list, but apparently even this local sophist refrained from doing so. The force of this *argumentum ex silentio* can moreover be tested by looking at the athletic contests, where local victors appear much earlier (Moretti Nos. for Elis: 1, 5, 60, 93, 114, 183, 284, 310, 318, 323, 337, Phigalia: 95, 99, 102, Lepreon: 267, 276, 309, 331, 338, Pisa: 15, Dyspontion: 2). Even if the earliest local victor(ie)s may not be historical, those from the 6th–5th centuries cannot be dismissed.

[124] WILL 1968, 70–71; LORENZ 2000, 103–105.

as the elite.¹²⁵ The relatively even distribution and (in comparison with Olympia) low numbers of the horse figurines all over Greece,¹²⁶ even in regions which were essentially well-suited for horsekeeping (e.g. Argolid, Thessaly), show that horsebreeding and the dedication of horse figurines were indeed restricted to the elite and there is nothing to suggest that it would have been otherwise in the case of Elis. In other words, the dedication of horse figurines does not reflect the large number of horses, but that of wealthy aristocrats. The large number of horse figurines cannot therefore result from purely or mainly local dedicators, since it is quite unlikely for Elis to have developed horsebreeding aristocrats in such extravagant quantities.

So, even if the exact reason for dedicating the animal figurines still remains mysterious, one can safely conclude that the majority of dedicators must have been foreign aristocrats visiting the sanctuary on a regular basis.¹²⁷ The number of dedicators could actually be reduced only if we assumed that they left several dozens of figurines at each visit of the sanctuary or that their visits were very frequent, i.e. occurring several times a year. In both cases it would be reasonable to suppose that the visitors were predominantly local ones. The dedication of multiple figurines (or the high frequency of dedicating single ones) could thus reflect the exceptional animal wealth of the surrounding region. This is actually the usual explanation discussed above, which postulates that the figurines were dedicated by the wealthy owners / herdsmen for the prosperity / fertility of their animals or for some other similar reasons. But as already pointed out, this *communis opinio* leaves several questions unanswered and is clearly not borne out by the evidence. There are no ancient testimonia attesting such a dedicatory practice in Greece and there are no ethnographic parallels either. This is all the

---

[125] MORGAN 1993, 23: „Horse figurines ...along with terracotta wagons and chariot groups reflect the pursuits of the wealthy; attempts to use chariot figures as evidence for early races are not wholly convincing."

[126] The Athenian Acropolis has produced approximately the same number of geometric horse figurines as the Thessalian sanctuary of Pherai. ZIMMERMANN 1989, 242–245 (listing 26 pieces from Pherai) and *ibid*. 269 (stating that 22 pieces come from the Athenian acropolis).

[127] The same view is already expressed succinctly by HERRMANN 1972, 72. Starting from a different consideration, the same conclusion has also been reached by EDER 2006, 554 n. 5: „Although dedications of bronze figurines in Olympia are neither rare nor especially valuable, representations of horse-drawn chariots and charioteers suggest that the medium of small bronze votives was chosen by elites to communicate messages of status and wealth."

more significant since cattle represent wealth in many other societies which were intensively studied by anthropologists dealing e.g. with the „African cattle complex".[128] There are naturally many differences concerning the rituals and customs connected to bovids, but the similarities with ancient Greece are equally conspicuous and were already described in detail.[129] Nevertheless, the production and dedication of animal images or figurines is absent in all the comparable cases[130] suggesting that the assumed practice at Olympia would be a unique phenomenon worldwide.

It is therefore hardly conceivable that local owners of horses and cattle dedicated animal figurines (whether few or many) and the traditional interpretation should be corrected. The main questions can thus be formulated in the following way: 1) Why did aristocrats living far away from the sanctuary develop the habit of dedicating animal figurines during the Geometric period? 2) What motivated the selection of this sanctuary? 3) What was the reason for the apparent exclusivity of Olympia? 4) Why was this special kind of dedicatory practice abandoned afterwards? By answering these questions, I hope to arrive at a conclusive explanation for the origins of the Olympic Games.

---

[128] For a summary see e.g. RUSSELL 2012, 301–304.

[129] MCINERNEY 2010, 26–32.

[130] The rock engravings and paintings in the Sahara showing large herds of domesticated cattle can perhaps be regarded as the only case, where typical pastoralists depicted their animals in a cultic context. Actually more than 60% of all art panels in the Sahara are reported to portrait cattle or cattle-related scenes. The purpose of these images and of the related ceremonial animal burials is far from clear (they might be connected to desiccation), but it is at least reasonable to assume that the practice was a direct continuation of earlier rock art created by foragers and depicting wild animals. Cattle imagery certainly seems to have gone out of fashion many millenia ago (DI LERNIA – GALLINARO 2010) and contemporary cattle herders in Africa do not use animal figures or images any more. Moreover the cattle scenes in the Sahara are distributed over a vast area and are not a similarly isolated phenomenon like the cattle figurines of Olympia in Geometric Greece.

Making Sense of the Evidence

The Archaeological Material

The problems connected with the tripod cauldrons and the animal figurines should be discussed together, because it is very likely that they were dedicated by the same group of people, i.e. by the well-to-do aristocratic elite of Geometric Greece. Now, the exact purpose and occasion of the dedication has to be determined and should offer a conclusive answer for the strange fact that these people have dedicated unpretentious, simple figurines along with the extremely costly tripod cauldrons. Moreover both kinds of dedications were made in extravagant quantities compared with the home-sanctuaries of the dedicators, and were far from their place of origin.

It was explained in detail above, the cauldrons were not just costly dedications, but were used for cooking in the sanctuary. What about the figurines? It is very likely that they were not primarily dedicated for representing the wealth or status of the dedicators (the terracotta ones are especially ill-suited for such a purpose), but presumably to fulfil some kind of ritual obligation. This would explain their large number as well as their relatively low cost, their often careless renderings and the variety of materials used, i.e. bronze as well as clay.[131] It remains to be asked, what this ritual obligation, i.e. the exact reason for dedicating the figurines, could have been. At this point, it is time to return to the identification of the figurines and by considering this, I hope to find a conclusive answer to these problems.

The cattle are conventionally described and interpreted as domesticated bulls and cows, but the position, the form and the size of their horns are strongly reminiscent of those of aurochs (Bos primigenius, Bojanus 1827): they are often inward-curving and the angle formed by the skull's axis and the horns is less than 60 degrees.[132] In addition they are much longer than those of domesticated cattle (Bos taurus). These features are not uniformly observable on all the figurines, but they occur very frequently and in all periods and workshops identified among them[133]. (*Fig. 2*) They are not restricted to the bronze figurines, but are equally

---

[131] A modern parallel could be the Fontana di Trevi at Rome.
[132] These are the characteristics enabling a distinction between the two species. See Appendix III and VAN VUURE 2005, 120–135 for further details.
[133] HEILMEYER 1979, Nos. 90–91, 230–236, 246–247, 383–386, 390, 391, 412–416, 511, 513, 583, 585, 763, 767, 774, 778, 781, 783, 826, 827, 856, 857, 881–889.

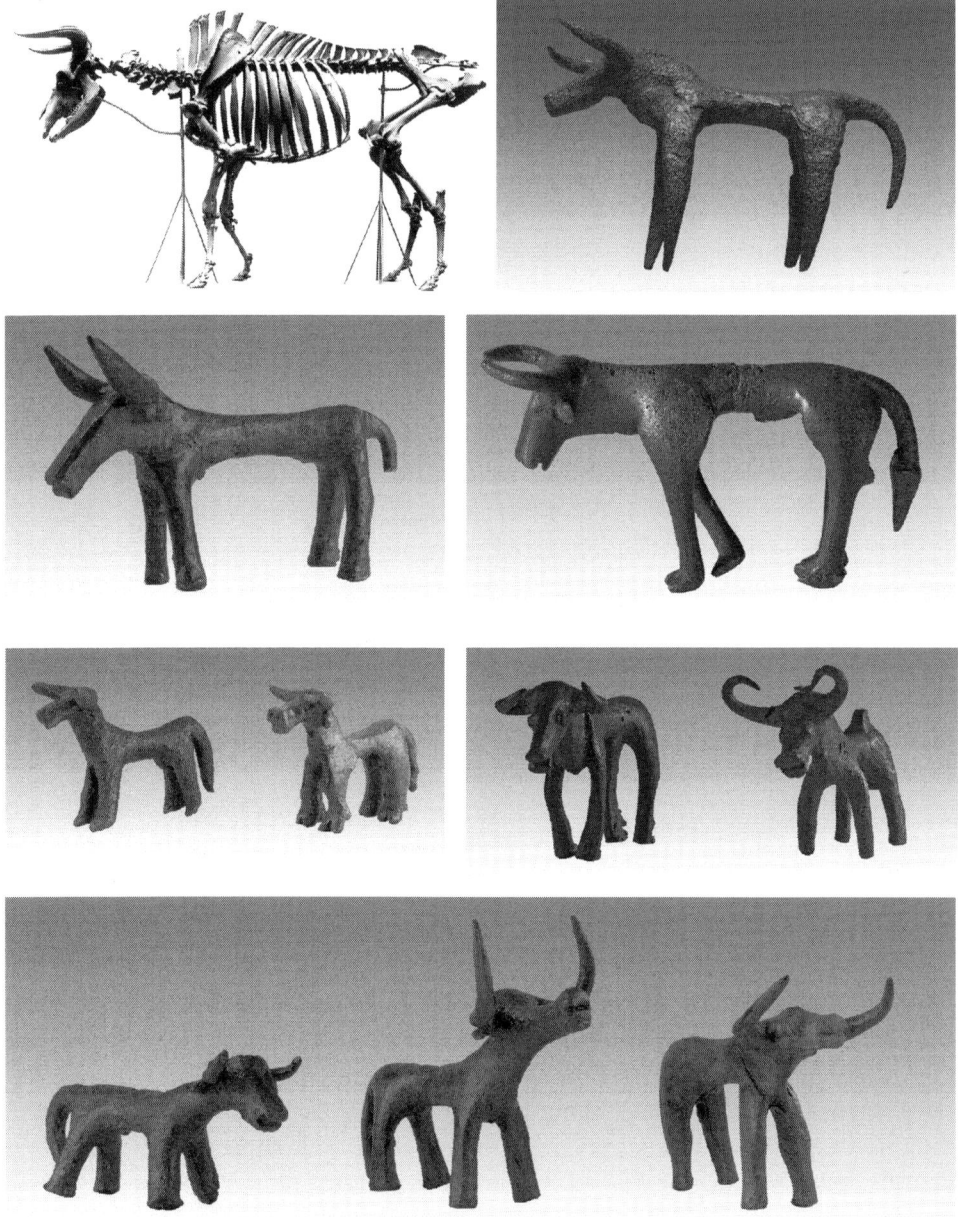

Fig. 2. Bronze bovine figurines found at Olympia (© Deutsches Archäologisches Institut, Athen) compared to the skeleton of an aurochs (Copenhagen Nat. Mus.)

present in the clay figurines dedicated at Olympia as well[134] and can be thus termed as constant features which are definitely not to be regarded as personal, regional or chronological idiosyncrasies. The resemblance to anatomical reality and the contrast with bovine figurines clearly depicting normal domesticated cattle in other Greek sanctuaries of the Geometric period[135] strongly suggest that the rendering of the bulls' horns at Olympia is not a general convention of Greek geometric art, but a realistic element of the otherwise schematically-modelled animals. After all, it is very likely that the horns, as the most important and distinctive parts of the animal, were depicted more carefully and rendered quasi realistically, while their bodies were treated more summarily. It is equally likely, given the mass production of the figurines, that some pieces were even executed carelessly in this respect.

Comparing the figurines from Olympia with depictions of ordinary domesticated cattle elsewhere in Greece, e.g. from those found at the Theban Kabeirion (*Fig. 3*), the formal differences are clearly recognisable and strongly suggest that they are not incidental.[136] An interesting difference between the two groups is discernible in their chronology as well: the series of bulls disappears from

Fig. 3. Bronze bull figurine from the Theban Kabeirion, ca. 6th century BC. New York, Metropolitan Museum

---

[134] HEILMEYER 1972, 124–125 ("Typenübersicht").
[135] See the pieces with known provenance (e.g. Delphi, Tegea and Lousoi) listed in Appendix II and the bulls of the Kabeirion.
[136] SCHMALTZ 1980.

Olympia after the geometric period, whereas they continue for several centuries at the Kabeirion.¹³⁷ This fact also supports the hypothesis that in Olympia the figurines represent not domesticated but wild animals and strongly suggests that their disappearance is not due to some change in the dedicatory practices, but can be explained by the extinction of the species resulting from excessive hunting and the spread of domesticated cattle in the region. It is after all these causes which led to the extinction of this animal in other periods and regions as well.¹³⁸

Moreover, even if there are no skeletal remains of aurochs in Olympia,¹³⁹ there is some osteological evidence for their presence on Crete, the only place where similar representations are attested in considerable quantities.¹⁴⁰ In addition to the famous cups from Vapheio, two passages in Homer can be interpreted as evidence for the presence of wild cattle in Greece and a gloss in Hesychius explaining a word as a special Laconian term for wild cattle shows that these animals were certainly present on the Peloponnese.¹⁴¹ In addition, the species may have found ideal conditions in the vicinity of Olympia and was likely to have been extremely rare elsewhere in Greece. By the time of Herodotus it seems to have been extinct in all Greece, but was to be found in Macedonia and its horns were still imported to Hellas.¹⁴² The bulls were certainly impressive in size and were surely regarded as exclusive game animals in Geometric Greece as well,

---

¹³⁷ The chronology given by Schmaltz has been criticized, especially regarding the date of his geometric pieces by LANGDON 1982, 596, but this revision would only emphasize the difference outlined here.

¹³⁸ VAN VUURE 2005, 72–78. For details see Appendix V.

¹³⁹ BENECKE 2006a, 2006b. For a general overview of wild and feral bovines in the entire Mediterranean see Appendix IV.

¹⁴⁰ PILALI 1985, 124 with references; PERSSON 1993; NOBIS 1996. The archaeozoological material dates from the Bronze Age, but it can safely be assumed that if the wild cattle did not become extinct during the peak of the Minoan civilization, they were likely to have survived during the dark ages as well.

¹⁴¹ Hom. *Il.* 12. 22–23; *Od.* 16. 295–296; Hesych s.v. κατράγοντες. For a discussion of the meaning of βόαγρια see TRÜMPY 1950, 36 and CHANTRAINE 1956, 46. Both argue for a meaning which would be independent of wild cattle (but nonetheless deriving from hunting), but are exclusively based on linguistic parallels and considerations which are not absolutely compelling and do not take the passage from Hesychius (let alone the material evidence) into consideration.

¹⁴² Hdt. 7.126 with KELLER 1887, 53–60; 1909, 341–343. For the distribution area and habitat of the aurochs see VAN VUURE 2005, 48–52; 245–258 or the excerpts in Appendix III.

since as their numbers were decreasing, the hunting of aurochs generally became a privilege of the aristocracy.[143]

Finally, ethnographic parallels can help to explain the numerous representation of the animals and the dedication of the images in a sacred place: the miniature figurines are used by hunters either as "Seelenfängerfiguren" in order to effect the successful catch or as thanksofferings for a god or goddess of the wild animals after the hunt effecting the regeneration of animals for the following hunt.[144]

Besides the many figurines clearly representing aurochs there are numerous pieces which do not have large horns curving inwards and look like ordinary domesticated cattle. If their numbers increased in later groups, one could take this as reflecting the gradual extinction of aurochs, due not only to hunting but also to the spread of domesticated cattle. But in fact there seems to be no such correlation and therefore I suggest another explanation. It is possible that the cattle represented were not always aurochs, i.e. genuine wild animals, but also feral ones, i.e. domesticated cattle which escaped and lived as wild animals for centuries. The horns of such bovines can be compared to the horns of most figurines (*Fig. 4*) and their osteological remains cannot be distinguished from their regular domesticated counterparts. Crossbreeds of wild/feral and domestic animals are also possible[145] and supposing that the manufacturers carefully depicted at least the horns of the animals, this could explain the large variability among the figurines as well. But in reality the bronzesmiths, most importantly those working outside the region, may often have had to produce the figurines without seeing the real animals or their trophies and so they simply relied on their autopsy of domestic cattle. Moreover, if the cheap figurines were merely used to fulfil ritual obligations and were dedicated in order to achieve success during the hunt, it is quite reasonable to assume that the dedicators were not much concerned with the rendering of the details.

The famous story of the herds of Helios on Thrinakia, as described by Homer, can be seen as a striking confirmation of the hypothesis outlined here. The episode is of central importance to the whole epos, and clearly shows that the consumption of cattle without human owners was considered a highly dangerous undertaking. The companions of Odysseus sacrificed the animals (even if not properly) and promised to compensate the god for eating them, but

---

[143] VAN VUURE 2005, 55–64 and Appendix IV.
[144] KARJALAINEN 1927, 5–6; HOLMBERG 1927, 83–99; 510–512; IVANOV 1958; PAULSON 1961, 27–35.
[145] Cf. VAN VUURE 2005, 167–168.

Fig. 4. Bronze bovine figurines found at Olympia (after FURTWÄNGLER 1890); feral cattle from the Camargue

were punished with death.¹⁴⁶ The offering of ἀγάλματα πολλὰ καὶ ἐσθλά would have been necessary in addition, as they themselves felt (*Od*. 12.347). Although the word ἄγαλμα in Homer does not mean 'statue' as in archaic or classical authors, but has a more general sense of 'pleasing gift, offering', in the present context ἀγάλματα are likely to be understood as figurines (representing either the animals themselves or their divine ruler), since in geometric sanctuaries this class of objects were common votive offerings and they were almost exclusively used as such.¹⁴⁷ The later development of the word's meaning is thus surely not

---

[146] The true nature of the herd as wild/feral cattle is not mentioned in the most recent commentary on the episode (MCINERNEY 2010, 93–95), but was pointed out several times earlier. VERNANT 1979, 240 puts it in the following way: "Sans être sauvages, elles ne sont pas non plus domestiques. Par leur appartenance au domain divine. Elles se situent en dehors ou au-delà de ces deux catégories. Sous la garde des dieux elles mènent une existence parfaitment libre et désœuvrée comme le font les bêtes sauvages; mais contrairement à ces dernières elles ne se dévore pas les unes les autres et vivent en troupeaux pacifiques." COOK 1995, 119 is more explicit: „the cattle which they slaughter are not domesticated, but belong to a god, are immortal, and have never been employed to plough the soil." HUGHES 2014, 89 calls these animals the „sacred wild cattle of the Sun-god Helios".

[147] COLDSTREAM 2003, 315: „More specifically votive are the figurines in terracotta and bronze; those in bronze, at any rate, are seldom found in any secular context."

incidental,[148] and the passage can be taken to illustrate the context of dedicating metal or terracotta figurines in the Geometric Age. As sacrifices and feasts based on ordinary domestic cattle are often described in the epic and no reference is made to offering ἀγάλματα, one can also assume that this was usually not practised. The near-absence of cattle figurines in most sanctuaries is in perfect harmony with this assumption. In the special case of Thrinakia, however, where the cattle were not of the ordinary domesticated type, the dedication of figurines in a sanctuary was considered appropriate.

So hunting or capturing wild/feral animals can be argued as representing the only explicitly attested occasion for dedicating animal statuettes in the Geometric Age and this practice could perfectly account for the mass dedication of bronze and terracotta bovine figurines at Olympia and for the similar practice on Crete. In addition, this hypothesis has the advantage of connecting the dedication of the animal figurines with that of the tripod cauldrons, which were clearly used to prepare the meat deriving from the hunted/captured animals.

The material from Crete, especially the most numerous group found at Kato Syme, can be adduced as a parallel and may serve for testing the above hypothesis. Geometric animal figurines disappear at this site roughly at the same time as in Olympia and since the worshipped deities and the artistic environment of the two sanctuaries are clearly different, it is unlikely that similar art historical or religious phenomena could have provoked the change in both cases. Instead, the decisive reason might be sought precisely in the hunt, which is clearly attested by the sheet bronzes as the central cult element in Syme during the later centuries.[149] It is most probable that this was the case earlier as well, the only difference being that the wild cattle became extinct and could not be hunted any more. Consequently the species was not depicted any more and dedicatory habits changed as well. Later

---

[148] For the meaning of ἄγαλμα see Lexikon des frühgriechichen Epos, Bd. 1, GÖTTINGEN 1979 and GERNET 1981, 113–114; von REDEN 2010, 157. The early attestations of the word in the epigraphic record are collected by KAROUZOS 2000, 12–22. In Homer ἄγαλμα is usually used in the singular, even if referring to more pieces (e.g. horses in *Od.* 4.602), the only other instance of the plural being *Od.* 3.274, where it has the general sense of 'votive offerings' and it is added that they were made of gold and textile. Other materials such as terracotta or bronze were presumably thought to be more usual. In the present context, we are only told that the many agalmata would be dedicated in the temple to be built, so they might be any kind of objects (e.g. jewellery) dedicated in a geometric sanctuary, but purposely-made offerings are more likely and in this case bronze figurines representing animals would be the most obvious choice.

[149] LEBESSI 1985.

literary sources clearly report that hunting played a decisive role in male initiation on Crete and this practice can definitely explain the dedication of hammered bronzes at Syme.[150] It is reasonable to assume that the initiation by hunting or the hunting itself did not start exactly with the appearance of the hammered bronze sheets, but originated much earlier and can therefore be used to explain the presence of geometric bronze figurines at the same site as well. Seen from this perspective, the remaining animal figurines at Syme appear to belong to the same context of hunting as well: wild goats were certainly game animals and the rams may equally have belonged to this category.

Pursuing this line of reasoning, one can find an easy explanation for the different kinds of animal figurines accompanying the bulls at Syme and in Olympia. The Cretan sanctuary was situated in a high mountain landscape providing optimal habitat for wild goats and rams, while the well-watered gentle hills and swampy lowlands around Elis and Olympia were ideal for feral horses. This is clearly attested by the Homeric epithet of the region, *hippobotos*, and in the famous story (Hom. *Il.* 11, 670–761) related by *hippota* Nestor.[151] Horses were of course not hunted to be sacrificed and eaten, like the aurochs, goats and rams, but they were presumably captured to be tamed and used as high-prestige domesticated animals.[152] This practice may have contributed considerably to the attraction of the region and may also explain the dedication of large numbers of horse figurines as well as the name and the prominent role of Hippodameia at Olympia. As the horses were captured and removed from their original living environment, a ritual restitution was considered appropriate, similar to the dedication of figurines representing ordinary game animals. In both cases, it was essential for the hunters to secure the procreation of the hunted or captured animals by mitigating the wrath of their former owner, the Master or Mistress of the animals.[153] The practice of dedicating bronze figurines of horses spread with

---

[150] Ephoros, FrGrHist 70 F 149 = Strabo 10.4.21; LANGDON 2008, 89–94.

[151] *Od.* 21.347 with MACURDY 1923, DELEBECQUE 1951, 39–42. To be sure, the epithet is applied to Elis only once, but ten times to Argos.

[152] In addition to the references above (note 123) see HODKINSON 1988, 64 „useless animal par excellence" (identical formulation by SALLARES 1991, 311; LANGDON 2010, 127).

[153] This might explain why the ritual restitution of the animals is a widely attested habit of primitive hunters as well: MEULI 1946, 935–1012. For the Master and/or Mistress of Animals see most recently MARINATOS 2000 and LANGDON 2010.

the animals and their new owners to other parts of Greece and to other sanctuaries as well.[154]

In this way the dedication of all geometric animal figurines can be explained more satisfactorily than by supposing owners or would-be owners of ordinary domestic animals making bronze dedications,[155] and the differences clearly observed between Syme and Olympia do not seem haphazard, but clearly reflect the different natural environments of the two sanctuaries. In this respect, a good parallel to the area surrounding Olympia is offered by the Rhône delta, where feral horses as well as feral cattle live together in the Camargue.[156] For the presence of feral horses around Olympia there are admittedly no literary testimonia[157], but feral cattle can be seen in the animals sacrificed by the Pylians in *Iliad* 11. 725–730 at the river Alpheios.

A general consideration points towards wild or feral animals around Olympia as well. Cattle are not easily movable for long distances, especially on such difficult terrain as the Peloponnese, so the animals sacrificed and consumed in the sanctuary must have originated from the vicinity. But in this case, supposing they were domesticated, one may wonder who their owners were and why these people would have allowed the visitors to slaughter their animals in the sanctuary. That there were private herds of cattle in this region seems to be evident and is explicitly mentioned by Homer, but the famous story related by Nestor also attests that these owners protected their herds vigorously. Generosity or hospitality seems not to have been characteristic of them, quite on the contrary: a *quadriga* sent to a race at Elis was retained by deception and only the charioteer returned to Pylos (*Iliad* 11. 698–702). So it is quite reasonable to assume that foreigners

---

[154] ZIMMERMANN 1989, 319–321 convincingly showed that the bronze horse figurines represent a speciality of the Peloponnese and were most probably invented just in Olympia. His contention that the bronze figurines originated from the clay ones is less secure. It is in my opinion equally or rather more probable, that the bronze figurines were made earlier and the terracotta counterparts represent only imitations or even cheaper substitutes.

[155] It was already pointed out for another context that „although subsistence was based largely on agriculture and herding, these subjects are notably absent from the art" (RUSSELL 2012, 19), but the observation seems equally valid for ancient Greeks as well.

[156] VAN VUURE 2005; DUNCAN 1992. See also Appendix VI.

[157] Feral horses are implied by the story about the origin of the Venetian breeds (Strabo 5.1.9) and closer to Olympia by the *aition* told by Pausanias (8.14.5-6) for a shrine of Artemis Heurippa at Pheneos.

could only feast in the sanctuary if they found wild or feral animals around it, or if they remunerated the owners. During the first centuries of the sanctuary, the first method seems to have prevailed, and after the extinction of the wild cattle, when they were replaced by domesticated ones, the second. This led to the increasing wealth and influence of the Eleans during the archaic period but certainly not earlier.

Regarding the disappearance of the figurines, the hypothesis of the extinction of the animals appears as a logical explanation.[158] Wild cattle were consumed on the spot during the feasts in the sanctuary, while the horses, which were more easily movable, were transported home by the visitors. For the *panegyris* the wild cattle were eventually replaced by their domesticated counterparts, but horse-breeding was hardly practised for a considerable time on a large scale.[159] The domestication made the ritual processes connected with the animals obsolete.

The general importance of hunting in the Dark Ages and afterwards in the Archaic period should be mentioned in this context as well.[160] It was proposed by Guggisberg that hunting lost its paramount place during the Geometric period and regained it only afterwards, but such a hypothesis of extreme fluctuation is clearly not likely and considering the above interpretation of geometric bronze figurines not necessary any more.

Finally, a few possible objections should be discussed. Cattle-hunting is not mentioned by Homeric epic, although hunting of other species plays a significant

---

[158] As HUGHES 2014, 102 already observed in general „Hunting reduced wild cattle, sheep and goats to remnant herds and eliminated them from some islands in Classical times. This was only one of a series of extinctions of island fauna." For the possible causes of these extinctions see also RUSSELL 2012, 176–186.

[159] In addition to the lack of winners in the hippic agons referred to above, our sources do not mention *hippeis* or cavalry in Elis before the 4th century (SPENCE 1993, 7–8). This fact may be regarded as not especially significant since cavalry forces are practically unattested in the whole Peloponnese during the 6th–5th centuries, but would be nonetheless quite hard to explain, if the numerous horse figurines had really resulted from horsebreeding practised on an unusually large scale here. The scarcity of horses might explain on the other hand the curious habit (Herodot 4.30; Paus. 5.5.2; Plut. *Mor.* 303b) of restrictions concerning mules in Elis. The few horses available had to be strictly protected and even though mules were needed (as they were much more usable for everyday purposes), they were bred only occasionally.

[160] For the importance of hunting in archaic Greece in general cf. e.g. Lane FOX 1996, SCHNAPP 1997, BARRINGER 2001. For prehistoric and Mycenaean Greece: HAMILAKIS 2003, for the Early Iron Age: BUCHHOLZ et al. 1973; EDER 2006, 553–554, GUGGISBERG 2008; LANGDON 2008, 252–255.

role in certain passages. Besides the general rule that absence of evidence is not evidence of absence, one can refer to the well-known fact that a Homeric reference to Olympia and to the Olympic Games is equally absent.[161] If cattle-hunting was practised only here and in connection with the cult, one should not expect to find a Homeric passage referring to it.

If cattle-hunting was really practised and was so fundamental for the dedication of the geometric bronze figurines, one might expect at least some of them to depict the actual hunt, i.e. the dogs attacking the prey, as is sometimes the case with contemporary deer. First, it is by no means clear that dogs would have been used in a cattle-hunt. If they were really employed, however, there are still, I think, two possible explanations for their absence among the figurines: if, as suggested here, the figurines were to represent the souls of the animals, in order to be able to catch and to kill them or to appease them afterwards and to effect their regeneration for future hunts, then the addition of dogs would have been plainly unnecessary. Consequently, their depiction in the case of the deer-hunt groups can be regarded as an exception rather than the rule, as their low numbers actually also suggest. From an art historical point of view, one can add that geometric art is highly conservative and artists are generally not eager to depict actions. The lack of cattle-hunt groups is therefore not so puzzling, and the exception, i.e. the groups of attacked deer, seem to be a relatively late invention, which would not necessarily have influenced the old and established tradition of other animal figurines.

In general, animal figurines are not a dominant class of dedications in major Greek sanctuaries. Especially after the Geometric period, statuettes or statues of animals on their own are rare compared to human or divine figures.[162] In contrast, animal figurines are often found in great numbers in shrines frequented by hunters and ethnographical observations made quite recently among Siberian peoples also furnish the underlying rationale: large number of wooden figures depicting fishes and animals were placed at sacred trees in order to effect the successful catch of

---

[161] As the region itself is often mentioned, this can not be fortuitous, even if the exact reasons for the silence are not clear.

[162] Horse figurines are by far the most common dedications representing animals, but horses were status symbols and this fact is most probably the reason for their relatively frequent depiction. The Kabeirion bulls or the terracotta ones near Chania referred to above (note 118) are clearly exceptional and most probably explained by cultic reasons.

the species.¹⁶³ A similar reason can most probably account for the appearance of numerous animal figurines at Kato Syme and there can be little doubt that the same applies to the stone reliefs depicting various kinds of animals at Göbekli Tepe. This site was recently discovered and identified as the very first temple complex and even if archaeology cannot provide conclusive proof concerning the dedicators and the occasion for the dedication, the connection with hunting can hardly be denied.¹⁶⁴ It is therefore quite reasonable to assume that hunters were generally inclined to depict their most important or prestigious game animals and that these animal images were often gathered at sacred places or sanctuaries from the earliest periods in human history until quite recently.

Here the general resemblance to paleolithic cave art might be considered as well. Although the exact purpose and meaning of these well-known and magnificent paintings is far from clear, it is absolutely certain that those who produced them, were hunters and that the depicted animals were wild ones and were usually hunted. Nevertheless, the actual hunt is never depicted and wounded animals are also represented only sporadically.¹⁶⁵ In general, the large number of animal depictions found at Olympia and Kato Syme may be compared to the large herds of animals covering the paleolithic caves and make the connection with hunting even more plausible. It is even interesting to note that the combination of bovids and horses is a constant feature of the prehistoric compositions, and that they always dominate the scenes¹⁶⁶ similarly to the geometric bronze figurines of

---

¹⁶³ KARJALAINEN 1927, 5–6.

¹⁶⁴ SCHMIDT 2006 and RUSSELL 2012, 62: "Göbekli Tepe is located on a limestone ridge far from water sources. It is a poor place for a settlement, but has an expansive view over the Harran Plain. No remains of houses have yet been found, but only public buildings with large T-shaped stelae depicting wild animals and, increasingly through time, humans. Fox bones are surprisingly prominent among the faunal remains, and foxes appear on the stone pillars. Fox and gazelle skins may have covered floors, walls, or benches in the structures, given the high proportions of foot bones in the assemblage. ... Some see these sites (i.e. Kfar HaHoresh in the Galilee Hills and Göbekli Tepe) as settlements of foragers contemporary and in interaction with nearby farmers, or as ritual centers for mobile foragers. However, Verhoeven argues convincingly that they are special-purpose ritual sites used by those farmers to carry out ceremonies focused on hunting and wild animals."

¹⁶⁵ In general see LEROI-GOURHAN 1992. According to him (*ibid.* 277–278) only some 4% of all the depicted animals are wounded (ca. 90 animals out of 2300) although different animal species and especially different geographic areas show different percentages.

¹⁶⁶ The constant combination of horses and bovins (aurochs or bison) is frequently described, e.g. by LEROI-GOURHAN 1964, 107–112. Horses represent ca. 30% and

Olympia. Local variations in the depicted fauna, like those between Olympia and Kato Syme, were also observed, in some caves the horses being accompanied by aurochs, in others by bisons.[167]

It is remarkable, however that „the species most abundant in the art are not those most abundant in contemporary faunal assemblages. This is true both at the global level – with reindeer and red deer dominating animal bone remains, whereas bison and horses appear most frequently in the art –and at the local level. In Cantabria, although both the most commonly depicted and the most commonly hunted taxa vary in different micro-regions, there is always an inverse relation between the two."[168] A similar situation is observed not only in the case of paleolithic cave art, but in widely different regions and periods (e.g. in Çatalhöyük) and seems to be true in general.[169] The artistic representations are therefore not to be connected with the regular subsistance hunt, but with special occasions, which already come close to sport hunting. The two are not always easily separated from each other, since hunting in general is typically (and especially if large animals are concerned) much more complex than a mere subsistence strategy, and sport hunting often retains many of the features of subsistence hunting.[170] It is therefore only natural that the aristocrats of early Greece who visited Olympia for the sake of sport hunting were eager to depict the animals similarly to their prehistoric predecessors.

In short, it seems to be a quite reasonable hypothesis that hunting wild/feral cattle and capturing feral horses represented the main attraction of Olympia and the sanctuary was initially a hunting shrine, similar to many other ones found all over the world.[171] Literary evidence also attests that the region around Olympia was an especially good hunting ground in later periods as well.[172] This hunting

---

bisons and aurochs together equally ca. 30% of all the depicted animals in paleolithic art, as counted by LEROI-GOURHAN 1983, 137.

[167] LEROI-GOURHAN 1992, 370–372.

[168] RUSSELL 2012, 14.

[169] Examples and further literature listed by RUSSELL 2012, 14.

[170] For a summary see Appendix VII with references in RUSSELL 2012, 155–168.

[171] In general, „it is striking that most of the elaborate hunting shrines are associated with agricultural groups. In these cases, the purpose of the shrines is less to assure a continued supply of a vital food source than to construct masculine identity by asserting a contrast to the domestic". (RUSSELL 2012, 64)

[172] Xen. *Anab.* 5.3.8-11; Paus. 5.6.6. As the wild cattle and feral horses became locally extinct by the end of the geometric period or shortly afterwards, it is not surprising that their hunting and capturing is not mentioned by the literary sources.

hypothesis offers an explanation for several curious features of the Olympic Games, which will be explored below.

The Basic Features of the Olympic Games

The most important basic features of the Olympic Games were their location and timing, both of which remained unchanged throughout antiquity. It is only to be assumed that place and time were fixed simultaneously with the first games and that they were not selected arbitrarily. However, no convincing explanation has been suggested for this choice. Starting from the above hypothesis concerning the origins of the games from hunting, a coherent explanation emerges.

First of all, it was hard to understand why it was precisely Olympia, obviously located pretty far away from all the main political centres of Early Iron Age Greece which attracted the most numerous and most valuable votive dedications, i.e. the wealthiest dedicators from the earliest times. Hunting as an aristocratic hobby *par excellence*,[173] which is often practised in remote locations, seems to be a convenient explanation. Moreover, it has already been observed that hunting is particularly prominent during periods of state formation and provides an important mode to display elite power.[174] As the highly valued wild or feral cattle were presumably only to be found in this region, the aristocratic hunters naturally selected this sanctuary to offer their dedications.

The usual explanation that the sanctuary was a neutral meeting place does not really explain the choice of this particular sanctuary, since many other could have been selected for the same reason as well. Moreover, it does not explain, how the visitors, arriving from widely different regions, could have come to meet each other and to enter into competition. Even in later periods, it was necessary to announce the exact date of the festival in order to make sure that everybody arrived approximately at the same time, but this practice of sending envoys can be practically ruled out for the earliest periods. The worshippers, i.e. the potential participants of the earliest contests must have been able to calculate the approximate date of the festival on their own. And the date itself was surely not selected arbitrarily but was connected with the rituals practised in the sanctuary. If the rituals which ultimately led to the establishment of the games were really connected to the hunt of wild bulls, the choice of the hottest summer months is

---

[173] In general see e.g. LANE FOX 1996; BARRINGER 2001.
[174] RUSSELL 2012, 165–168.

perfectly logical: this is the rutting season of these animals which are in other periods living separately from the cows and therefore not easy to locate. During the rut, however, they become readily visible and it is precisely this period of the year which is traditionally preferred for hunting animals with a similar behaviour (e.g. the deer).[175]

It is also a strange fact that the festival coincided with the full moon.[176] The light of the moon was regarded in antiquity as dangerous and it is therefore not surprising that most festivals generally avoided the middle of the month, when moonlight was most visible.[177] On the contrary, hunter people are inclined to attribute a positive character to the moon and the Eskimo even assume that the spirit of the moon governs the game animals. If their numbers fell significantly and more were needed, the shamans would visit the moon and ask him for more animals.[178]

Concerning the individual contests, it has already been noted that according to literary tradition the only event was for a long time the stadion race, but this detail was considered dubious, since the event was unspectacular, and as the Homeric poems attest it was not even very popular and certainly was not worth a long journey on its own. It was therefore conjectured on the basis of the many athletic events described in Homeric epic that there were, from the beginning, other competitions as well, which were, however, not recorded or not acknowledged for some reason.[179] In addition it was argued above that these missing competitions were different from those which were introduced and practised later on. Hunting

---

[175] VAN VUURE 2007, 264–271. The rutting season of aurochs in Poland was in late summer (August and September), but in the Mediterranean, this must have come earlier: in the Doñana National Park (Spain), the mating season of wild cattle comprises June, July and August.

[176] This is the meaning of διχόμηνις, a main characteristic of the festival emphasized already by Pindaros (3 Ol. 19) Cf. Schol. Pind. 3Ol. 35d: ἐπεὶ ἐν τῇ πανσελήνῳ ὁ Ὀλυμπιακὸς ἀγὼν ἄγεται, καὶ τῇ ἑκκαιδεκάτῃ γίνεται ἡ κρίσις.

[177] In Athens, it was only the Dipolieia, with its old-fashioned ritual of the *bouphonia*, which was celebrated on the 14th of the month Skirophorion. Other main public festivals were timed either at the beginning or the end of the months. The Lenaia, Anthesteria and Thesmophoria fell approximately in the middle part of the months, but were all over by the full moon and did not involve public animal sacrifices on a large scale but chthonic and fertility rituals. Cf. DEUBNER 1956.

[178] HAASE 1987, 60–62. It is perhaps worth noting that according to the most recent studies moonlight can really influence the behaviour of several animal species and is especially relevant for foraging primates: KRONFELD-SCHOR *et. al.* 2013.

[179] E.g. GARDINER 1925, 87–88; HERRMANN 1972, 80–81.

as the very first kind of sporting activity is therefore the best possible candidate to fill this gap. That the athletic contests were introduced only later and, as our sources state, gradually because the hunt was becoming increasingly difficult and was finally abandoned altogether, is completely reasonable. It is only to be asked, why precisely the short distance run was selected first or why this has become the very first contest at the games. If the games evolved from a ritual similar to the *staphylodromia* at the Karneia, as suggested here, then the answer is quite clear: the race had its origins in the ritual chase and was therefore naturally the very first athletic discipline.

That hunting was intimately connected with some kind of running in early Greece is clearly demonstrated by Ephorus (*apud* Strabo 10. 4. 20),[180] who records that it was precisely these two activities which were closely supervised in the Cretan education system obviously preserving some very old customs.[181] The ritual chase and subsequently the running contest was most probably performed after each successful hunt (or at the end of the hunting season), as part of the ceremonies celebrated in honour of the dead animal, a practice which is well-attested among various peoples and is referred to as „animal ceremonialism".[182] This hypothesis can be further substantiated by looking at the ritual prescriptions connected to the Olympic Games.

Ritual Prescriptions

The use of crowns made of wild plants, the anointing of one's body, sexual abstinence before the contests and athletic nudity were already interpreted as ritualized behaviour deriving from pre-hunt activities practised by primitive hunters. The theory remained controversial and is certainly not acceptable in all

---

[180] ἑκάστης δὲ τῆς ἀγέλης ἄρχων ἐστὶν ὡς τὸ πολὺ ὁ πατὴρ τοῦ συναγαγόντος, κύριος ὢν ἐξάγειν ἐπὶ θήραν καὶ δρόμους, τὸν δ' ἀπειθοῦντα κολάζειν. „the leader of each "Troop" is generally the father of the assembler, and he has authority to lead them forth to hunt and to run races, and to punish anyone who is disobedient" (English translation by H. L. Jones).

[181] The importance attached to running is further demonstrated by the fact that according to the law code of Gortyn adult citizens with full legal capacities were designated as *dromeis* in contrast to the younger *apodromoi*. See WILLETTS 1955, 11–14; BILE 1992, 13.

[182] PAULSON – HULTKRANTZ – JETTMAR 1962, 74–75, 93, 385–386. The most elaborate ceremonies are directed towards bears, which were already collected and discussed by HALLOWELL 1926. Cf. Appendix VIII.

respects, but seems to point in the right direction.[183] The usage of oils against body odour certainly remains a very attractive explanation and may well originate from hunters' practices, since it is vital for the hunter to eliminate his own scent. But oils were actually applied by Greek athletes everywhere and its usage was not specifically enforced at Olympia, so even if this feature is really explained by ritualization of certain procedures observed by hunters, it is most probably not especially relevant for the origins of the Olympic Games.

Athletic nudity may be more pertinent, since it was allegedly introduced exactly at the Olympic Games at a very early date.[184] Our earliest source (Thuc. 1.6.5), however, explicitely referred to this as a relatively new development initially practised by the Lacedaemonians and even though it is possible to assume that it actually originated from Olympia, the aetiological stories about its introduction are likely to be late speculations rather than historical records. Admittedly, the athletic nudity is very likely to have derived from wearing loincloths only, a practice which is widely attested among hunters,[185] but similarly to the anointing of one's body, this has nothing to do specifically with Olympia and its games.

There are, however, two ritual features which can be safely regarded as specifically and exclusively connected to the Olympic Games: the crowns given to the winners and the exclusion of married women. We have no firm evidence on the age of their introduction and can simply observe that the other Panhellenic games imitated the use of crowns, while had no prohibitions against women. The wild olive crowns thus certainly predate the beginning of the 6th century BC.,[186]

---

[183] SANSONE 1988, most recently criticized by MURRAY 2014.

[184] Dion. Hal. 7.72.3 attributes the invention to the Spartan Akanthos, Paus. 1.44.1 and many others relate it to Orsippos from Megara. All the sources agree that the date was the 14th or 15th Olympiad, but this information is of course not to be taken at face value. For more details see PETERMANDL 2013.

[185] SANSONE 1988, 101–115. It should be pointed out that for runners it is not the presence or absence of a loincloth which is decisive, but the footwear and it seems to be symptomatic that all the running events at Olympia and elsewhere in ancient Greece were held barefoot, which is typical for hunters but unusual in real athletics or in competitions detached from cult: at the Mandan foot race in north Dakota, which was described as „Olympic in character", runners were „entirely naked except for their moccasins" (CULIN 1907, 808), while Ishi, the famous last representative of an indian tribe, was proud of his shoes, but did not wear them during hunt, because they made a noise and thus deterred the prey (SANSONE 1988, 113).

[186] According to Phlegon (FGrH 257 F 1. 10), the prize was originally an apple and has been changed to the wild olive wreath only subsequently. This isolated piece of evidence is, however, unlikely to be true historically.

but the exclusion of married women is also unlikely to represent a late addition.[187] Both may be seen as relics of the most ancient cult practice at the sanctuary and corroborate the idea that the Games evolved from hunting.

First of all, it is remarkable that, judging from the Homeric epic, winners of athletic games were generally rewarded with valuable prizes, while at Olympia there were no awards apart from the crown of the wild olive tree. It is easy to understand that once established at the most prestigious games, this practice came to be imitated in other sanctuaries as well, but how it became an accepted custom contrary to the general trend is a much more difficult question. It is reasonable therefore to suppose that the high popularity of the games resulted not only or not primarily from the intangible prestige of the games (which would be quite unexpected for a new establishment), but that winners won some prize which was materially valuable even without the organizers offering it. Valuable prizes could have been offered by the participants themselves, but later on this was not practised at all. So, the possiblity is rather strong that the valuable goods won by the successful participants were game animals and that the crown was just a distinction marking the favourite of the gods at the feast where the game animals were consumed.

Furthermore, the wild olive tree providing the victor's crown was certainly not typically connected with Zeus,[188] like the oak in Dodona or the white poplar in Olympia[189], and other deities do not seem to have a special relationship with this tree either. However, the only other grove of wild olives is attested on a hill which was crowned by a shrine dedicated to Artemis (Paus. 2.28.2-3) and

---

[187] As the rule does not appear at the other Panhellenic Games, it was likely to be irrelevant in the case of athletic sport events or at least unimportant from a practical point of view (women did not often travel in general, and the wives of the competitors most probably remained at their distant home anyway, without any particular prohibition). It is more likely that the prohibition was an age-old taboo, inherited from the predecessor of the games and was obsolete already during the archaic period and was therefore ignored in the other games.

[188] Already WENIGER 1919, 32–40 connected this tree with the cult of Gaia.

[189] For the oak at Dodona see WENIGER 1919, 11–16. White poplar was the only kind of tree which was allowed to be used on the great ash altar of Zeus at Olympia (Paus. 5.14.2), but this regulation is likely to derive from the poplars close connection with Heracles. This tree was usually associated with the underworld and it was not typically connected to Zeus but to Heracles (BÖTTICHER 1856, 441–444).

Artemis was certainly often associated with different kinds of trees.[190] The sacred *kotinos* was called Kallisto[191] and in Arkadia Artemis Kalliste was venerated in a shrine standing on the supposed tomb of Kallisto, surrounded by many wild and cultivated trees (Paus. 8.35.8). Moreover, at Troizen Artemis was linked with a wild olive tree and hunting (Paus. 2.32.10). The cultic prominence of Artemis at Olympia was noted already earlier[192] and the region was certainly a superb hunting ground (Xen. *Anab.* 5.3.8-11; Paus. 5.6.6). So one is entitled to suppose that the wild olive tree at Olympia was originally sacred to Artemis and hunting played a major role in her cult. It is even probable that originally the festival and the games were celebrated in her honour. The centre of the sanctuary, the main ash altar of Zeus, was always and exclusively constructed with the water of the river Alpheios (Paus. 5.13.11), which has no obvious connections with Zeus, but is intimately linked with Artemis (Paus. 5.14.6 and 6.22.8). It is therefore logical to assume, in accordance with the archaeological evidence outlined in Appendix IX, that the ash deriving from the sacrifices was originally sacred to Artemis and was integrated only subsequently in the cult of Zeus.

The exclusion of married women, while girls were allowed to be present as spectators,[193] points in the same direction. The reason for this regulation, which is clearly a religious taboo, has been searched for in vain: the explanation based on the cult of Demeter[194] is totally unsubstantiated and the other attempt seeking a derivation from the cult of Herakles[195] is equally unsatisfactory because it is based on two unwarranted assumptions, i.e. that the sanctuary had been established for the sake of holding sports events and that the cult of Herakles was more ancient than any other at this site. In fact, the exclusion of married women is

---

[190] Paus. 3.16.11 (Orthia called as Lygodesma as well); 8.13.2 (Kedreatis). Already FARNELL 1896, 429 supposed that Artemis was especially connected with wild trees.

[191] Schol. Theocr. id. 4.7. The most detailed discussion is still WENIGER 1895.

[192] Pausanias mentions seven altars for Artemis (5.15.4-7; 5.18.8), a number which is second only to the ones dedicated to Zeus. Cf. also WENIGER 1907, 96–114; SOLIMA 2011, 127–139; HEIDEN 2012.

[193] DILLON 2001, 237–239. The assertion (*ibid.* p. 106 and 238) that women in general were barred from the Olympic Games is erroneous, since Pausanias 6.20.9 explicitly states that virgins were theoretically not excluded from watching the games. KYLE 2007, 225–228 argues for the admission of *some* virgins as a special privilege and quite correctly concludes that „even if virgins, in general, were not banned from the male games, realistically, they were not there."

[194] DREES 1962, 119–124.

[195] MOURATIDIS 1984, 50–54.

unattested in any cult of Zeus, but there is a direct parallel in the cult of Ephesian Artemis,[196] which strongly suggests a derivation from the cult of Artemis.[197] And since the separation of adult women is widely attested among hunter-gatherers[198] the practice ultimately derives in all probability from hunting practices.[199]

It is significant that all the available evidence points to the importance of hunting and can be seen as a corroboration of the hypothesis that the Olympic Games evolved from ceremonies connected with this special kind of activity. It remains to be asked, how and why hunting was eventually replaced by athletic contests. I attempt to answer these questions by looking at the origins of the penteteric periodicity of the Games.

The Penteteric Periodicity

Ancient tradition unanimously states that from their very beginning the Olympic Games were celebrated, like their modern successors, every fourth year. This penteteric periodicity was the rule in the case of many other ancient festivals (*panegyreis*), but the underlying reasons and circumstances of its adoption are far from clear and have, as far as I can see, not attracted much scholarly attention recently,[200] although they might be expected to have been fairly important. As the

---

[196] Artemidor, *Oneirokrit.* 4.4 and esp. Achilleus Tatios 7.13. In other cults, there are no similar regulations attested. cf. FEHRLE 1910.

[197] In Greek mythology, this goddess was always accompanied by young girls, who were banned from her if they had lost their virginity; her cult demanded chastity from her priestesses as well. Cf. e.g. KAHIL 1984, 618–621 and Paus. 7.19.1-6; 7.26.5.

[198] FRAZER 1911, 190–204; BURKERT 1979, 118; SANSONE 1988, 52–54; RÖHRICH 1993, 397. For details see Appendix VIII.

[199] A practical reason for the exclusion might be that the scent of menstrual blood is demonstrably repelling herbivores, especially ungulates such as deer (March 1980). The taboo on menstruating women is most widespread among hunters than any other people (KITAHARA 1982).

[200] I see e.g. no discussion of the subject in DECKER 1995, AUFFARTH 1998, SINN 2000, 2002, CHANIOTIS 2011. There was one elaborate or rather sophisticated explanation put forward by WENIGER 1905, which is rarely cited explicitly (CORNFORD 1927, 229–230; DREES 1962, 110–118), but seems to be still influential (DREES 1967, 39). Ziehen 1939, 2–3 refuted Weniger's arguments and concluded: "Wenn nach der antiken Ansicht die penteterische Feier schon der ältesten Zeit angehörte ... so ist das für uns unannehmbar. Denn es muß als ausgeschlossen gelten, daß die astronomische Erfahrung und Gewandtheit, die immerhin eine penteterische Ordnung voraussetzt, schon so früh in Olympia zu Hause war. Es ist an sich denkbar, daß die Olympien

discussion will show, it does not belong either to the basic features of the games from the very beginnings, nor is it a ritual prescription.

Ancient literature provides only one mythical explanation (Paus. 5.7.9), which actually shows that the real reasons were unknown even in antiquity. In general, it is hardly conceivable that the festival was penteteric from the outset, because the program, the rules, the number of judges, i.e. practically every detail concerning the games, have been changed,[201] so it is unlikely that only the periodicity remained constant for nearly a millennium. Admittedly, there are some instances where a festival was celebrated with a penteteric periodicity probably from the very beginning, but in these cases it was always the organizer who determined and enforced this rule.[202] A powerful mythical founder (e.g. Herakles) was easy to imagine in the Classical period, but would be quite anachronistic in the Early Iron Age, characterised by petty chiefs and by a large number of isolated communities[203] and would moreover not explain in itself the reason why the penteteric periodicity had been chosen. Ancient authors dealing with the origins of the Olympic Games also developed another, more sophisticated hypothesis, that the Games had been established by a covenant concluded by the Spartan Lykourgos, Iphitos of Elis and possibly Kleosthenes of Pisa.[204] Such a

---

ursprünglich einmal sogar jährlich gefeiert wurden, wenn auch nicht durchaus regelmäßig. Wahrscheinlich ist, daß vor der penteterischen eine oktaeterische Ordnung bestand." For more recent discussions or rather passing remarks see e.g. BRELICH 1969, 453–454, LÉVÊQUE 1982, 8, MORGAN 1990, 43; BURKERT 1992, 81.

[201] For a historical summary of the changes in the program and the number of the judges see Paus. 5. 8.6- 9.6. Cf. GOLDEN 1998, 41 table 4. The judges were called hellanodikai only from the second quarter of the 5th century BC; their earlier designation being diaiteter (cf. e.g. SIEWERT 1999; MINON 2007, 532–533). As already mentioned above, athletic nudity was not the rule from the beginning either.

[202] The only case where the periodicity is explicitly attested from the very beginning as penteteric is the Delia instituted by Athens (Thuk. 3.104), the other Athenian penteteric festivals (Her. 6.87 and *AthPol* 54.7) might have been converted from annual celebrations. The festivals mentioned by Strab. 5.4.7 (Neapolis); 7.7.6 (Nikopolis); 17.1.10 (Alexandria) are likely to have been penteteric from the outset. The only case where the participants themselves were supposed by ancient sources to have determined the periodicity at the founding of the festival were the Eleutheria (Plut. *Arist.* 21), but this foundation story is historically unreliable (cf. SCHACHTER 1994, 138–143 and most recently KONECNY 2012, 28 n. 100, 37 n. 172) and the decision was most probably made also in this case by the organizers.

[203] MORGAN 1990, ULF 1997b.

[204] Plut. *Lyk.* 1.2; Phlegon (FGrH 257) F 1. 2.

written treaty in the 9th–8th cent. BC. is equally unrealistic for several reasons, and can therefore definitely be ruled out as a source for the penteteric periodicity, even if it was purportedly documented on a bronze disc conserved in Olympia.[205] Nevertheless, it seems to come nearer to the reality, for it is reasonable to suppose that it was some kind of a gentlemen's agreement between the participants and local organizers which ultimately determined the periodicity. However, this agreement must have been based on negotiations and was likely to undergo some changes as the group of participants was not constant either. This consideration strongly suggests that the festival was not always penteteric and certainly not so from the outset,[206] but it does not tell us, if it was celebrated more often or rather more sporadically, and may even lead to the assumption of irregular (or continuously changing) intervals.

Literary tradition states that the games consisted originally of a single event, the stadion race and the victors list suggests that the competitors came from the neighborhood i.e. from the Peloponnese.[207] If we trust these pieces of information, one may conclude that at the beginning the festival was a local event of relatively minor importance and was celebrated similarly to other harvest thanksgivings most probably annually.[208] Actually, even if one is not confident about the reliability of the traditional victor list and about the authenticity of the single stadion race,[209] the annual periodicity can still be regarded as the most likely assumption, since the Olympic Games were part of a religious festival which were most often celebrated annually. Moreover, there are indeed some

---

[205] Paus. 5.20.1. Cf. SINN 2002, 178; NAFISSI 2003, 33–34. The authenticity was defended for the last time in detail by HÖNLE 1968, 7–13 and accepted by GAUER 2000, 118–119.

[206] As supposed by BRELICH 1969, 454. The reason for this assumption is the initiatory character of the games, a hypothesis which is simply not borne out by the evidence: mere participation in the games was not valued and was frequently repeated, success was promised only for a very few participants and it was, according to tradition, common practice that the participants were first mature men and boys were admitted only afterwards.

[207] See in general: MORETTI 1957.

[208] The annual rhythm is explicitly advocated for various reasons e.g. by CORNFORD 1927, ZIEHEN 1939 and MALLWITZ 1988. SWADDLING 1980, 12 succinctly connected the origins of the games with harvest festivals, implying but not stating the annual periodicity. Similarly, the rural character of the early cult is widely accepted (most recently e.g. TAITA 2009, SINN 2010), but the periodicity is usually not discussed.

[209] DECKER 1995, 43; CHRISTESEN 2007.

penteteric festivals, which are reported by ancient sources to have evolved from annual celebrations.[210]

For the annual celebrations there is also an archaeological corroboration: The wells dug into the soil of Olympia were evidently necessary for providing enough drinking water in the heat of the summer for a relatively large crowd of people, and according to the ceramic finds discovered in these wells, A. Mallwitz concluded that they were first dug around 700 BC. Now, it is likely that the reason was the reduction of festival frequency causing the appearance of larger crowds at the same time in and around the sanctuary. Assuming that the first 25 games were annual, we arrive at about 700 BC. for the first one.[211]

There is, however, an alternative hypothesis, that the penteteric periodicity derived from an octaeteric cycle.[212] For the Olympic Games were not celebrated simply every fourth year, but at an interval of 50 or 49 months resulting, according to a widespread hypothesis, in a cycle of 99 lunar months, which is equal to 8 solar years with the festival falling alternately in Apollonios or Parthenios.[213] This hypothesis has been challenged with good reason and it is more likely that the alternation of 49 and 50 months was not regular.[214] Moreover, even if octaeteric festivals are known from Delphi and Sparta,[215] there is no evidence that the Olympic Games were celebrated with this frequency at any period. This can be definitely ruled out before the traditional foundation date and is equally unlikely before ca. 700 BC., because the underlying calendar system was of oriental origin and most probably adopted by the Greeks only during the orientalizing period.[216] The very system of alternating months, was most probably unknown to Pindaros (3 Ol. 35) or to his contemporaries, and one can safely assume that the octaeteric cycle applied for computing the date of the festival was the result of a long evolution rather than the starting point of the system. So it is impossible to assume an octaeteric frequency for the earliest games (unless we postulate a much later inception and a lower total of games than traditionally) and annual celebrations remain the most likely hypothesis.

---

[210] CHANIOTIS 2011, 13. The most important one is the Panathenaia, the periodicity of which is discussed in detail by BRULÉ 1992, 24–25.
[211] MALLWITZ 1988.
[212] DREES 1962, 113; LÉVÊQUE 1982, 8; BURKERT 1992, 81.
[213] Schol. Pind. Ol. 3. 35a. Vgl. HANNAH 2005, 37–39.
[214] MILLER 1975.
[215] Plut. Quest. Graec. 12; Plut. Agis 11.3. Cf. RICHER 1998, 155–171.
[216] NILSSON 1962, 47–51.

Two questions remain open even in this case: 1) why was the original frequency changed at all and 2) why was the selected frequency precisely a penteteric one.

For the first one, it was only Mallwitz, who tried to find an answer. He assumed that the annual rhythm of the first games was abandoned and that the penteteric periodicity was adopted because the chariot races were introduced at the 25th festival (Paus. 5.8.7), so that transporting the chariots every year to the location of the games would have involved very high costs for the owners.[217] It was correctly objected, however, that chariot owners were particularly wealthy and not driven by economic considerations, as shown by the introduction of several equestrian games in the festival circuit, which were regularly attended by the same aristocrats.[218] Besides this hypothesis does not offer an answer for the second problem, i.e. it does not explain why the new frequency chosen was a penteteric one. This is a serious disadvantage, because considering the equestrian contests introduced at the beginning of the 6th century, a biennial/trieteric rhythm could be expected: this frequency was the rule at the Nemean and Isthmian games from the outset and it has never been changed, but at Olympia there are no signs of this frequency. So the entire explanation can most probably be ruled out.

The reason for adopting the penteteric rhythm is often sought in the octaeteric cycle. As the octaeteric frequency is unlikely to have preceeded the penteteric one and did most probably not represent the original system, this hypothesis cannot account for the change of the basic annual system and does not seem to be a compelling reason for the subsequent adoption of a penteteric festival either. Obviously, a trieteric festival could equally have resulted from it (as in the case of the Nemean and Isthmian games) and on the other hand, there were some other regularly recurring events which used the penteteric frequency but had surely nothing to do with the Olympic Games or with the octaeteris.[219]

Astronomical and logistical considerations proposed so far are therefore not likely to have played a decisive role in determining the frequency and do not explain the change from the annual celebrations. I think therefore, that other explanations should be looked for.

As already mentioned, there were some religious festivals held annually, which were, however, celebrated more lavishly every fourth year. The most well-known example is the Panathenaia, but the Karneia of the Dorians was most

---

[217] MALLWITZ 1988.
[218] LEE 1988, 114.
[219] Herodot 3.97; 4.94. Diod. 5.32.

probably of the same type. In contrast, the Olympic Games were celebrated only every fourth year and annual festivals were lacking.[220] This difference should be stressed and requires some kind of explanation, since otherwise there are striking similarities between Karneia and the Olympic Games.

How are these to be interpreted? As already mentioned, it is unlikely, that the Karneia would have influenced the Olympic Games or *vice versa*, since the athletic games and the sanctuary are not an exclusively Dorian establishment and there is no apparent reason why the Olympic Games should have influenced only the Dorians in such a way. Some kind of common origin seems to be more plausible and the clue lies, I think in the running event, which is so conspicuous in both. Now, the *staphylodromia* was a chase and it can be reasonably supposed that the stadion race developed from a similar ritual, since its most important mythical aition, the chariot race between Oinomaos and Pelops is also basically a hunt or chase and not a real race, as it is conventionally called. For the chase practised at the *staphylodromia* there are several ethnographic parallels,[221] and these unequivocally show that the pursued person actually represented some kind of animal, so the ceremony can be most conveniently called a ritualised hunt. As regards hunting, one can observe that it is intimately connected both with the origins of Greek athletics in general and specifically with Olympia as well: as already mentioned, the vicinity of the sanctuary was renowned as an especially good hunting ground and Artemis, the goddess of wild animals and hunting had more altars in the *altis* than any other divinity apart from Zeus.[222] This exceptional cultic popularity of Artemis in and around Olympia was noticed long ago and the correct explanation, i.e. that she was venerated as the goddess of the hunt, was also offered for the phenomenon.[223]

---

[220] DREES 1967, 24 mentions two passages that could attest a small annual festival of Zeus, but ZIEHEN 1939, 46 already noted that these are insufficient to prove annual festivals for Zeus at Olympia. The most explicit source cited by both Ziehen and Drees as „Anecdota graeca, ed. Siebenkees, p. 95" (a misprinted page number in the quoted edition instead of 59) is actually a scholion on Plato *Phaedr.* 236 b 3 (= K. F. Hemann, App. Plat., Leipzig 1875, 267): „ἔνθα τὰ Ὀλύμπια καὶ ἀγὼν πενταετηρικός, Μουνυχιῶνος μηνὸς ἤγετο τῷ Διί, ... ἤγετο δὲ καὶ κατ' ἐνιαυτόν, ἅπερ ἐλάττω ἐκάλουν".

[221] WIDE 1893, 76–77.

[222] For Skillus as an exceptionally good hunting ground: Xen. *Anab.* 5.3.8-11; Paus. 5.6.6. For the cult of Artemis Strabo 8.3.12 C 343 and WENIGER 1907, 96–114; SOLIMA 2011, 127–139.

[223] WENIGER 1907, 98.

As noticed above, the exclusion of married women is also paralleled only in the cult of Artemis and this fact strongly implies that the *panegyris*, which was celebrated penteterically in honour of Zeus, was orginally a festival for Artemis and retained an important ritual prescription even after the change of the honoured deity. A striking confirmation of this hypothesis can be seen in the fact that while there is no annual *panegyris* attested for Zeus at Olympia, Strabo (8.3.12 C 343) explicitly mentions more than one for Artemis. In this way the curious absence of annual celebrations could be explained as well: the penteteric festival emerged from the annual celebrations in the usual way, i.e. retaining the annual ones, but after a while the honoured deity changed from Artemis to Zeus.[224] Hunting, which was the core of the festival, gradually disappeared and was finally abandoned altogether, while athletic contests evolving from the running ritual practised after each successful hunt, began to be held as a replacement. These phenomena, i.e. the change of the honoured deity and the change in the cult practice (abandonment of the hunt and emergence of the athletics) must have occurred at approximately the same time and were surely closely related to each other.

Now, one might of course ask, what the reason for these changes could have been. The answer is, in my view, quite simple: the intensification of hunting attested by the rapid growth of votive dedications in the sanctuary during the 8th century BC[225] (and presumably the spread of agriculture as well) reduced the number of game animals dramatically. And because it was impossible to raise more of them or to reduce the number of the hunters, hunting became unpredictable and often unsuccessful. This might explain the divergence of the annual and penteteric celebrations. For a certain period, hunting was still feasible, but success became increasingly rare, i.e. wild/feral bulls were caught only irregularly, e.g. every other or third year. When the species became extinct, hunting continued with other game animals at the annual festival of Artemis Elaphia, and the wild cattle were replaced by domesticated ones at the festivals celebrated at larger intervals.

---

[224] Such a change is by no means impossible, as the same festivals were celebrated in different poleis for different gods. AUFFARTH 1998, 488: "Zudem ist kaum ein Fest exklusiv nur mit einem Gott, umgekehrt sind Feste gleichen Typs mit unterschiedlichen Göttern verbunden." That the ashes of the sacrificial victims had to be mixed with the water of the Alpheios, closely connected to Artemis and that the procedure was restricted to the month Elaphion (Paus. 5.13.11), suggest an intimate connection between the great altar of Zeus and Artemis.

[225] MAASS 1978, 228; HEILMEYER 1979, 21–23.

Following this change, there was of course no point in retaining the tutelary goddess and another deity could be chosen.

It cannot be determined exactly when this change occurred,[226] but the reason for choosing the penteteric periodicity can be discerned quite clearly. For it cannot be mere coincidence that already by the time of Homer, it was common practice to sacrifice a four-year-old (*pentaeteros*) ox or bull for Zeus.[227] The reason for this is simply, as already pointed out by the ancient commentaries,[228] that the animal is then at its peak, and this is therefore the best time to slaughter it. At a large *panegyris*, however, some younger animals must have been killed as well in order to provide enough meat for all the participants, but precisely because of this it was reasonable to let some time to pass without slaughtering or sacrificing afterwards in order to raise the numbers again. The exact period necessary to compensate for the loss caused by the mass slaughter at a *panegyris* depended on several factors, but considering the low reproduction rate and the maturation of bovids at the age of 1.5–2 years, the minimum interval practised was one of two years (i.e. to skip the year following immediately the *panegyris*).[229] But if it was the goal to provide the largest possible number of sacrificial animals at a single occasion and at regular intervals, without considerable risk of diminishing their total number, then the penteteric periodicity had to be chosen, since a shorter interval would have meant less animals and waiting for more than four years would have been obviously uneconomical. The interval thus resulting between two *panegyreis* was certainly sufficient to regenerate the herds and it is therefore not surprising that this periodicity was adopted for the two largest Panhellenic festivals at Delphi and at Olympia.

It is therefore likely that the penteteric periodicity is not derived from astronomical considerations i.e. from the octaeteric cycle, but from biological and economic constraints dictated by the animal sacrifice practised at the

---

[226] The penteteric frequency must have been adopted as a rule during the 7th century, because at the beginning of the 6th century, it was already well-established and adopted by the Pythian games and shortly afterwards by the great Panathenaic festivals as well.

[227] *Il.* 2.402–403; 7.313–315; *Od.* 19. 420–423.

[228] Arist. *Hist. Anim.* 575b.5.

[229] This principle led to the trieteric periodicity observed at Nemea and Isthmia and it was retained apparently because the number of participants and attendants did not rise to such a high level as at Olympia, so it was not necessary to slaughter all the animals available.

festival.[230] The basic principle of leaving more than a year's interval between two celebrations derived from hunting, the precise interval of four years was fixed on the basis of animal husbandry. As the system was of the first importance for the sustainability of the festival, it was retained afterwards without any change and was often adopted in other similar cases as well. The penteteric rhythm thus evolved from the gradual extinction of the game animals and this process also led to the introduction and increasing importance of athletic contests. Finally, as the special wild animals disappeared, the hunt was replaced by the sport events.

---

[230] MANNHARDT 1905, 533 has already envisaged a similar reasoning for the origins of the penteteric periodicity of the gallic festival reported by Diod. 5.32: "augenscheinlich nur wegen der vorzüglich reichen und kostspieligen Ausstattung des vielleicht von einer ganzen Eidgenossenschaft mehrerer Stämme gefeierten Festes war die Feier aus einer jährlichen zu einer pentaeterischen geworden." The parallels listed by Mannhardt show that according to local differences, large agricultural festivals may be celebrated regularly but at very different intervals.

Pelops and the Origins of the Games

Contrary to previous discussions, the mythical tales about the earliest games have been deliberately neglected so far, but after the analysis of the archaeological material and the related rituals, an attempt can be made to return to this subject. After all, it would be most strange if there were no myths reflecting somehow the real origins of the games, and indeed the tales about Pelops seem to fit the „hunting hypothesis" outlined above very well, even if this is not apparent at first glance.

Strictly speaking, Pelops was usually not considered as a founder of the games in antiquity; he was just one of the many reorganizers, the more important founders being Herakles (either the Theban or the Idaean) or Iphitos.[231] But the myths surrounding him are intimately and almost exclusively connected to Olympia[232] and therefore it is a fair assumption that these tales reflect somehow the origins of the games as well.

The myth of Pelops is made up from two distinct parts, which are not closely related to each other in our extant sources[233] but were likely to have formed a coherent narrative[234]: (1) the resurrection from the cauldron and (2) the winning of Hippodameia by defeating Oinomaos in the chariot race.[235] Previous attempts at elucidating the genesis of the myth and its connection with ritual practices (most commentators concentrating on either the first or on the second part of

---

[231] ULF 1997a.

[232] HERRMANN 1980 assumed on the basis of scattered references found in Strabo and Pausanias that the mythical home of Pelops was rather in the NE Peloponnese than in the neighbourhood of Olympia. This assumption is rather improbable, since there are absolutely no earlier references to connections between Pelops and this region, while the report of Strabo and Pausanias may well be based on late traditions. On the islands of Pelops in the Saronic gulf, see below n. 272.

[233] Pindaros, the only one, who attempted to create a link between them in his first Olympic ode, did so by explicitly declaring the cauldron story as false, even though he ostentatiously referred to the vessel and to the shoulder blade of Pelops in his 'true' version as well. Cf. NAGY 1986.

[234] This assumption will be substantiated below in detail. It is, of course, much easier to assume, as done most recently by EKROTH 2012, 96 that „the mythic background of Pelops is diverse and inconsistent."

[235] This sequence of the two episodes seems to be fixed in the ancient sources, but as the discussion below will show, originally it was most probably the other way round.

the myth without attempting a coherent interpretation[236]) reached very different and apparently inconclusive results[237], and because it is of central importance for the Panhellenic sanctuary at Olympia it is worth reconsidering the case. First the chariot race is analysed by gathering different parallels, and the possible connection of the two episodes is considered only afterwards, followed by a tentative reconstruction of the historical development based on the objects recovered from the soil of the sanctuary. Pindaros' aims, methods and intentions in his first Olympian ode, which are so often discussed in this context,[238] are irrelevant for the present argument, because it is intended here to deal exclusively with the period preceding this poem.

---

[236] NAGY 1986 and HUBBARD 1987 are the only ones who attempt this. Nagy declares both parts as an aition for the Olympic Games (for the footrace and for the chariot race respectively), Hubbard tries to explain the Oinomaos episode as a logical extension of the cauldron story, similar to the hesiodic myth about Prometheus, Epimetheus and Pandora, but although the structural similarities in general seem to be close enough, they are especially weak regarding the chariot race. (Cf. HALM-TISSERANT 1993, 145–151.)

[237] The myth is usually discussed in connection with the Olympic Games and both are considered to derive from some kind of initiation ceremony (e.g. NAGY 1986, HUBBARD 1987). This idea is based on BURKERT 1972, 108–119 accepting the interpretation of the chariot race proposed by DEVEREUX 1965 (a work which is otherwise barely cited) and dealing practically exclusively with the cauldron story. The theory of Devereux (connecting the mythical chariot race with taboos surrounding a curious habit in animal husbandry observed in Elis, (cf. Herod. 4.30; Paus. 5.5.2) is therefore of fundamental importance and its basic problems deserve to be mentioned here: the real reason for the taboo is not explained (in general, some sort of pastoral rites are assumed, but such a hypothesis is highly unlikely, since there are no parallels for the custom observed at Elis, and a specific reason in Elis is not given either), the cauldron story is dismissed altogether and possible parallels for the chariot race are entirely left out of discussion. Another, quite isolated attempt at interpretation is represented by BUTTERWORTH 1966, 135–145 and ELIADE 1968, 68–69 who connect the cauldron myth with shamanistic initiation practices. The dismemberment, cooking in a cauldron followed by resurrection often appears in fairy tales and finds evidently very good parallels in shamanistic initiations (see PROPP 1987, 112–118), but the derivation of this motif from prehistoric initiation rituals is not a likely proposition: RÖHRICH 2002, 380–381.

[238] E.g. NAGY 1986, KRUMMEN 1990 and GANGLOFF 2012 (discussing other authors and social, political aspects as well).

It is assumed that the cauldron episode, which has many parallels in Greek mythology and ethnography in general,[239] is the older or original part and that the story of the chariot race was only added when chariot races became established at the Olympic Games (ca. 680 BC).[240] But actually chariots were certainly represented much earlier at Olympia, and although I agree that they are not to be connected with local chariot races, they might reflect not only the status of the dedicators (in which case they should be found in comparable numbers in other regions/sanctuaries as well), but local myth or cult practice involving chariot teams as well. There is therefore no decisive argument for a secondary addition of this part or for the primacy of the other one, and it is reasonable to assume that originally they were somehow connected – even if not exactly in the same way as presented by Pindaros in his first Olympic ode.

It is not surprising that the cauldron story was more often discussed than the chariot race, which seemed to be closely or even exclusively connected with the Olympic Games and was even regarded as an aition for the games in general or for the chariot race in particular.[241] But actually there is a striking parallel for the famous race of Pelops and Oinomaos, which is mentioned only sporadically[242] and which shows that this is not necessarily true: the footrace, by which the suitors of Atalante were challenged. In both cases the basic plot is the same: there is a beautiful girl, who can be won only by winning an impossibly difficult race, in which the suitor either loses his life or wins the bride. After a large number of unsuccessful attempts, the one who eventually wins is aided by a god and uses a trick. So far, the story follows a familiar structure of folktales,[243] but contrary to the usual pattern, even though the bride is won, the resulting marriage is not a

---

[239] SCHMIDT 1963, 113–155; BUTTERWORTH 1966, 137–142; UHSADEL-GÜLKE 1972, 22–30; PROPP 1987, 114–115. For more details see Appendix X.

[240] BURKERT 1972, 113–114; 1988, 35–37.

[241] It was only Butterworth and Devereux, who sought its origin in a different realm, but the theories did not find a wide acceptance. Apart from BURKERT 1972, 110 n. 11, Devereux is only mentioned by WEILER 1974, 211 n. 429, but even in this case, it is not cited for its main thesis. Butterworth is never cited, except for CANOSA 1994, 56–58.

[242] As far as I can see, besides PROPP 1987, 408, who explicitly but very briefly refers to both contests in the same context, it is only FRAZER 1911, 299–301 and WEILER 1974, 256–258 who discuss them together, declaring that they both belong to the type of matrimonial contests, widely attested around the world.

[243] PROPP 1972, 64–65, 1987, 436. A nice parallel is given by PROPP 1987, 406: the daughter of the tzar is running a contest with her suitors. If one of them is able to overtake her, she will marry him, those who fail, hovewer, lose their heads.

happy one and the story ends in divine punishment for the couple or domestic strife – and, in the case of the Pelopids, even in a curse that pursues the descendants as well.[244] This unhappy ending is not unique in Greek mythology (e.g. Theseus and Ariadne or Iason and Medeia can be seen as parallels in this respect), but there are some specific, significant and perfectly matching details, which thus connect the myth of the chariot race and the footrace: Atalante gives a head start to the suitor, as Oinomaos does, and the severed heads of the many unsuccessful suitors are similarly displayed so as to deter future candidates.[245] The only difference is that Pelops drives a chariot, whereas the suitors of Atalante have to run, and that it is Atalante herself who kills the unsuccessful suitors, and not her father.

It is unlikely, that the two stories influenced each other directly, it is rather to assume that they can be regarded as two variants of the same theme. What can be learned from their comparison? First of all, it is to be asked, if the designation 'race' is correct at all. It has already been noted[246] that in the case of Atalante, the race, as it is conventionally called, seems originally to have been a chase, and the mythical chariot race is also more of a chase than a real race. But actually it might have been the case that a race was transformed in these instances into a chase. The question can be answered only if it can be clarified what the race or chase was really about.

It would seem that the main theme in both cases was marriage. All who have dealt with the subject have adduced as parallels the mythical footrace for the daughters of Danaos and the historically attested wooing of the daughter of Kleisthenes at Sikyon, as well as other athletic contests observed by ethnographers for „determining" the bridegroom. The hypothesis has been that a similar custom

---

[244] Chrysippos, an illegitimate son of Pelops was killed on the instigation of Hippodameia, who committed suicide (Hygin. 85) or moved to Midea to escape the wrath of Pelops (Paus. 6.20.7).

[245] Hygin. 84.3 (Oinomaos) and 185.2 (Atalante). The usage made of the heads in adorning or building a temple is early attested for Oinomaos (Sophokles fr. 432) and Euenos (Bakchylides fr. 61). The similarity with the suitors of Atalante has been noted only by GUIDORIZZI 2000, 465 n. 871. Others (GRUPPE 1906, 839, n. 1.; CORNFORD 1927, 219–220, WEILER 1974, 135 n. 29) have referred only to the similar practice attested for Antaios (Pind. Isthm 3/4. 70–71), Euenos, Phorbas, Diomedes and Kyknos, all of which are conveniently assembled by ancient commentators (Schol. in Pind. Isthm. 4.92a; Tzetzes in Lykophr. Alex. 160). The motif is well attested in fairy tales of different cultures (but not all over the world) and seems to be employed specifically and exclusively for the unsuccessful suitors of a mythical bride: GOBRECHT 1996.

[246] WEILER 1974, 191; FONTENROSE 1981, 176.

prevalent in the early phases of human history would be reflected by the myths.[247] But the unhappy or rather sinister ending of the two mythical stories actually precludes this conclusion and shows that the rape of the bride is just a traditional motif employed in a different context. Moreover, it should be emphasized in contrast to all the adduced mythical and ethnographic parallels that, in the case of the Pelops and the Atalanta myths, it is not the bride who is pursued by the suitors, but the suitor by the bride or by her father. This basic structural difference has generally been overlooked[248] and strongly argues for a different interpretation and origin of these two particular myths. If they were both derived from the widespread motif of bridal contests,[249] there was probably some specific reason for the most unusual structural inversion, or we have to assume that the structure of the tale has remained unchanged even after a superficial assimilation to the bridal contest. The second possibility seems to be more plausible, but in any case it is very likely that the connection with marriage is not of primary importance and that both myths represent some kind of chase or flight rather than a race

---

[247] WEILER 1974, 257 following FRAZER 1911, 301. The parallels among the Kirghiz and Calmuck (FRAZER *ibid.* 301–302), where the bride has to marry the suitor who overtakes her, may seem at first especially striking: although the girl is not running, but riding on horseback, she is equipped with a whip, so that she can ward off the unwelcome suitors, who are approaching her. (The same ethnographic examples were used by MCLENNAN 1865, 181–184 as evidence for the primeval tradition of capturing women from another community.) The parallels cited from german speaking peoples, where Brautlauf often denotes a footrace, in which the competitors are no longer the bride and bridegroom (*ibid.* 303–304), are less compelling.

As for the real relevance of an athletic contest in determining the bridegroom, the ethnographic parallels are not conclusive. They show, that it was not merely the speed of the suitor that was decisive in the race, since it is often remarked that the chase was a mere „matter of form" or „usually a pretence", and among the Koryaks, the whole ceremony was arranged in such a way, that the suitor „has little chance of succeeding unless the girl wishes it and waits for him". (FRAZER *ibid.* 302) At any rate, the better known case of Agariste clearly demonstrates that in reality it was not a single athletic event, and not even the athletic performance or speed which determined the future bridegroom. If this had been intended, Kleisthenes could easily have selected one of the olympic victors. But actually he did not really care about athletic excellence and simply used the festival to announce his invitation, i.e. took advantage of the presence of many possible candidates. I doubt in general that any real father would decide about the marriage of his daughter simply by the outcome of a race.

[248] FRAZER 1911, 301 has perhaps realised this when he cautiously states that the story of Atalanta is „somewhat different from these traditions".

[249] FRENZEL 1987 often refers in this context to the myth of Pelops and Hippodameia.

for the bride. The myths concerning the rape or abduction of a bride (Idas – Marpessa, Iason – Medeia), which are structurally also closely related to the myth of Pelops and Hippodameia, are similar in this respect: there is absolutely no race or contest, only a chase, in which the father of the bride (Euenos, Aietes) tries but finally fails to catch the couple.[250]

The „brides" point in the same direction: Atalante, the virgin huntress, was rightly considered as a variant of Artemis, and Hippodameia equally seemed to be a heroine derived from a divinity.[251] The goal of the chase was primarily to catch and to kill the „suitors", who on the other hand tried in both cases to escape. If they succeeded in this, they won the (favour of the) virgin (deity). As the pursuer was in the case of Atalante a huntress par excellence, the chase can be plausibly called a real hunt, implying that the virgin goddess was the mistress of the wild animals, and the pursued „person" was meant actually to be an animal.[252] At any rate, the strong connection of the myth with Artemis is clearly shown by the tradition that the grave of Hippodameia's suitors (along with the bones of Pelops) was allegedly located in a shrine of Artemis Kordax at Pisa (Paus. 6.22.1). And that the outcome of the chase was in most cases fatal for the chased „suitors" whose heads were displayed like trophies of veritable game animals,[253] is consistent with this hypothesis, however absurd it might seem at first.

First it is worth noting that the rape of a human bride through an animal is a widely attested motif of fairy tales and is nothing exceptional in itself.[254] The assumption that animals and humans were not strictly divided in early human

---

[250] As noticed long ago (TAMBORNINO 1930, 1917), Idas, Marpessa and Euenos (Apollod. 1.59–60) can be regarded as exact doubles of Pelops, Hippodameia and Oinomaos. It is probable that the story known from Olympia was adapted in this case to account for the name of the river Euenios. A similarly late derivative (Sithon and his daughter Pallene) is discussed by WEILER 1974, 217–219.

[251] Atalanta: FONTENROSE 1981, 177, RENAUD 2004, 312–313; Hippodameia: BEVAN 1986, 205–206.

[252] BUTTERWORTH 1966, 140 also assumed that Pelops was identified with an animal ancestor of the Pelopidae, "which seemed to have been the horse." SCHMIDT 1963, 152 on the contrary, made the following suggestion: "Pelops ist wohl auf der Stufe knapp vor der Begegnung des Tantalidenhauses mit den Olympiern noch theriomorph gewesen. Es war wohl ein göttlicher Schafbock, dem da in Pisa schwarze Widder geopfert wurden."

[253] Hyginus *fab.* 84.3 and 185.2.

[254] In general see THOMPSON 1958 B 600–699. For a collection of Greek mythical examples see ROBSON 2002.

thought is clearly reflected by many tales in which humans and animals confront each other as equals (i.e. they understand each other and can marry and have children).²⁵⁵

The similarities with the myth of Sedna, an important mistress of the wild animals, which is well attested among contemporary hunter-gatherers of the arctic region may be adduced as a general corroboration of the idea as well. Here Sedna is said to have been a young girl reluctant to marry, who is eventually abducted by some kind of animal. Her father either kills her husband or tries but fails to rescue her from the unhappy marriage, and Sedna eventually becomes the mistress of the animals and of the nether world.²⁵⁶ The similarities with the myth of Hippodameia are obvious and striking, and it is clear that the myth is not primarily concerned with marriage. In a similar way, human virgins are often depicted in myth as brides for the quarry of the hunt.²⁵⁷

The assumed identification of Pelops with an animal is also in perfect harmony with the other part of the myth. The best ethnographic parallels for the boiling and resurrection of Pelops from a cauldron concern in fact not human figures but animals,²⁵⁸ and even in Greek mythology there is the tale in which the cauldron is successfully employed for the resurrection of an animal but fails to rejuvenate the human Pelias. This latter name seems to derive from the same root

---

²⁵⁵ BREDNICH 1977, 592–594, DALGAT 1979, 756–757, BAUER 1993, 428. The genesis of mankind out of animals and stories about animals changing their appearance in human beings is also widely attested.

²⁵⁶ FISHER 1975; HAASE 1987, 54–58 (with previous literature) and Appendix X. The difference that it is often the animal-husband, who pursues the father and his daughter and that Sedna dies during the chase, does not seem to be especially important. The marriage of Pelops and Hippodameia also ends in a rather similar way (cf. above n. 244) and there is a clear parallel in the myth of Hyrnetho, to whom a grove of wild olive trees was dedicated (Paus. 2.32). Hyrnetho was also abducted in a chariot by her brothers and pursued by her husband and eventually lost her life during the chase.

²⁵⁷ BURKERT 1972, 76 n. 25 listing several examples and previous literature. Detailed description of a single case (blackfoot indians) in ROBSON 2002, 67–68.

²⁵⁸ UHSADEL-GÜLKE 1972, 28–29; RÖHRICH 1993; PUCHNER 2002 and selected examples in Appendix X. The most striking parallel, which has also been termed as a doublette of the myth of Pelops, is about Thor and Thjalfi in the Edda cf. SCHMIDT 1963, 127–128. It is notable that in the famous story of the „Machandelboom", the dismembered and cooked boy is resurrected to his human form only after being transformed to an animal.

as that of Pelops[259] and therefore the connection with the cauldron is unlikely to be a mere coincidence. The implication is, that Pelops, who could be resurrected from the boiling cauldron, was not a human figure, but an animal. The name Pelops is especially revealing: similar personal names, like Dryops or Merops are mythical ancestors of certain tribes (Dryopes, Meropes), but at the same time denote animals.[260] That eating from a cauldron may have the effect of turning a man into an animal (as assumed in the rituals on mount Lykaion)[261], points to the same direction. The last famous myth concerning the boiling and resurrection from a cauldron is the orphic myth of the infant Dionysos[262] and it is remarkable, that this god was definitely identified, and exactely in Elis, with an animal, the bull.[263]

The famous shoulder-blade of Pelops, eaten by Demeter and replaced by the gods in ivory has already been connected with the fact that this bone played an important part in animal sacrifice and probably even had divinatory functions.[264] The motif of the missing part (often a bone) is an important and widespread element of similar resurrection stories occurring almost exclusively with

---

[259] Already GRUPPE 1906, 145 considered Pelops and Pelias as two variants of the same name (cf. KRETSCHMER 1938, 5). A different etymology seems out of question. The name Pelopeia occurred in both families and Pelias is even referred to by Paus. 5.8.2 as one of the founders of the Olympic Games. The similarities could not be stronger.

[260] Their etymology is uncertain, most probably ungreek (e.g. Thracian or Illyrian), but similar names with a clear greek etymology are also known: Dolops – Dolopes. Pelops and the hypothetical Pelopes, who were assumed on the basis of the name „Peloponnese", belong most probably to this group. von KAMPTZ 1982, 45–46, 139. For the etymology of Pelops see below note 292. Different kinds of animals with names ending in –ops (but not used as ethnica) include e.g. πάρνοψ/κόρνοψ (locust), πηνέλοψ (wild duck), δρύοψ (woodpecker), ἔποψ (hoopoe) or μέροψ / εἴροψ / ἀέροψ (bee-eater) σκάλοψ (blind-rat) and certain fishes (ἔλλοψ, σέσοψ, αἰθίοψ).

[261] BURKERT 1972, 98–108, JOST 1985, 249–269.

[262] DETIENNE 1977, HALM-TISSERANT 1993, 165–172.

[263] Plut. mor. 299B (PMG 871) with BROWN 1982. Plut. Isid. et Osir. 35 (mor. 364 F) refers to tauromorphic statues of Dionysos among the Greeks and the god was occasionally called „son of a cow" or referred to as having horns. Cf. FARNELL 1896, Vol. V. 126 and 284 with note 34; DIETRICH 1974, 116–117.

[264] BURKERT 1972, 115; GROTTANELLI 1984, 855; ZOGRAFOU 2005, 137. Only PUCHNER 2002 is sceptical in this respect. The importance attached to this bone is clearly reflected by the legend concerning its magical power in the Trojan war (Paus. 5.13.4-7) and by its alleged healing capacity (Plin. Nat. Hist. 28.34). Later on, even the Trojan Palladion was thought to be made of this bone: Clem. Alex., Protrept. 4.47.6; Arnob., contra gent. 4.25; Firm. Mat., adv. pag. 15.1-2. (cf. ZOGRAFOU 2005, 136–143).

animals[265]. The fact that it was thought in antiquity (Paus. 5.13.5) to be larger than lifesize strongly suggests that the famous bone of Pelops actually belonged to an animal that was larger than a human figure.[266]

Moreover the name of the mythical persons cooked and resurrected from a cauldron may plausibly be seen as referring to wild animals: Arkas, the grandson of Lykaon, cooked by the latter for the gods, was clearly (even if etymologically incorrectly) associated with the common indoeuropean name of the bear[267]; Melikertes, the son of Athamas, thrown in a boiling cauldron and resurrected afterwards as Palaimon, can equally be seen as denoting a bear, disguised in a way which is typically used by hunters and with a name often applied to this dangerous species.[268]

Last but not least, the geographical term Peloponnese, attested for the first time during the 7th or 6th century,[269] does not necessarily imply an anthropomorphized Pelops. This sense is certainly intended by Tyrtaios (frg. 2), and Thucydides (1.9) explained the name of the peninsula in this way as well, but this rationalistic interpretation is not likely to be correct. There are a few similar geographical terms which show that animal names were often employed for islands,[270] while other personal names (especially those of the the most famous heroes) are not attested in

---

[265] The only exception is the "Haselshexe". SCHMIDT 1963, 113–155; UHSADEL-GÜLKE 1972, 28–29.

[266] MAYOR 2000, 104–110 supposed that the bone actually was a fossil, originally perhaps belonging to a mammoth. The theory would explain the large size of the bone, but Pelops is never described as a giant or monster (as are other mythic creatures, convincingly related by Mayor to fossil finds), and since there are many other and apparently richer fossil deposits on the Peloponnese, a single piece in Olympia does not seem to be a sufficient ground for attracting much interest in antiquity.

[267] The etymological derivation from arktos is uncertain (FRISK 1973, 142, BEEKES 2010, 133 s.v. arktos; following SOMMER 1934, 63–64), but not impossible and ancient tradition clearly connected Arkas and Arcadians with bears. Cf. BURKERT 1972, 105–106; BORGEAUD 1979, 48–49.

[268] It is beyond doubt that the name Melikertes is connected etymologically with honey, although the exact meaning is unclear (LESKY 1931, 519). The substitute name for bear, which is widely used for tabooistic reasons in many languages is precisely the honey-eater: RÖHRICH 1993, 397–398.

[269] Kypria fr. 16.3-4 (West); Tyrt. frg. 2 (Bergk).

[270] Strab. 13.2.5 (C 618) already collected similar island names (Prokonnesos and Myonnesos) and one might also add Elaphonesos (Scylax, *Peripl.* 94) as well. Pithekoussai is morphologically different, but semantically clearly a good parallel. The same is true for Euboia as well. Looking at other toponyms, not just island names,

similar composita.²⁷¹ Islands or other geographical formations (mountains, lakes etc.) bearing the names of mythical or historical persons (e.g. Pillars of Hercules/ Gibraltar) are rarely attested in general²⁷² while the invention of mythical or pseudohistorical persons based on toponyms is much more common.²⁷³ The case of the Csepel island on the Danube (to the south of Budapest) seems to be a very close parallel: already during the Middle Ages it was reported to be named after a certain man of this name, but actually the word is very likely to derive from a common noun meaning 'bush'.²⁷⁴ A similar derivation of the human Pelops from the Peloponnesus is very likely.²⁷⁵

The anthropomorphisation and hero cult of Pelops should be discussed in this connection as well. In the earliest extant literary source (Hom. *Il.* 2.104–105) Pelops already appears as a human ancestor of the Atreids, but given the severe anthropomorphism of Greek myths, this is no surprise after all.²⁷⁶ Since Homeric epic does not exactly mirror the actual reality or the religious concepts

---

one can equally find many names deriving from animal names, like Kynoskephalai, Aigospotamoi, etc.

[271] The islands of Aiolos (Thuk. 3.88) seem to be the sole exception, but even in this case the individual islands had other names.

[272] The 9 small islands in the Saronic gulf off Methana mentioned by Paus. 2.34.2 as the islands of Pelops may belong to this category. This isolated piece of evidence is usually taken by Herrmann 1980 to refer to the mythical Pelops, but this interpretation is not particularly likely. Pausanias was certainly interested in Pelops (5.13.7), and wherever he mentions this hero in an unusual location, he gives some details. In this case, he fails to do so (actually he mentions only a strange meteorological observation), and this might suggest that the islands had nothing to do with the mythical Pelops, but were named relatively recently after some historical person, who bore this name. (Pausanias 6.10.3 reports that an island was named after a historical person, Glaukos of Karystos, the famous pugilist and not after his mythical namesake.) From the hellenistic period the name Pelops enjoyed a certain popularity (GANGLOFF 2012, 97–98) and Pelops, son of Alexandros, a Macedonian in the service of Ptolemy II is a particularly good candidate for this (cf. AMELING 2000).

[273] E.g. Paus. 3.1 where Eurotas and Taygetos are also mythical persons along with Lakedaimon, Sparte and Amyklas. Paus. 3.14.2 also mentions a certain Tainaros, giving the name for the famous cap.

[274] BENKŐ 1966.

[275] The etymology and meaning of the word Pelops will be discussed below n. 292.

[276] KIRK 1974, 50–52.

and practices of the dark ages,[277] and because it is well-known that a Homeric reference to Olympia and to the Olympic Games is missing, the Homeric passage mentioning an already human Pelops does not necessarily exclude the possibility that the name originally denoted an animal. As Homer and Hesiod were credited already in antiquity (Herodotus 2.53) with assigning the gods their names and describing their forms, epic poets may have equally invented or transformed heroic figures. Homeric animals are very close to the heroes in general[278] and the name Pelops resembles other animal names. Moreover animal names like Keleos/Dryops/Merops[279] or Karnos/Krios[280] clearly show that it is perfectly possible to attach the name of an animal to a mythical human figure. The hero cult of Pelops was long supposed to be a very old one at Olympia, but most recently a more reasonable view emerges, which seeks the origins of this cult around 600 BC. at earliest.[281] It was also during the second half of the 7th century that the geographical term Peloponnese was interpreted for the first time as the island of a famous hero, Pelops by Tyrtaios (frg. 2). This accords perfectly with the view expressed here, that Pelops as an anthropomorphic hero made its appearance only after the Geometric Age when due to the extinction of the wild bulls, hunting of this species was not practised any more.

Finally a biblical parallel should be perhaps mentioned. The intended sacrifice of Isaac by Abraham (Gen. 22) has already been discussed in this context by Grottanelli, who actually assumed that a completely different attitude towards human sacrifice is attested by the two tales: in Genesis, the sacrifice of one's

---

[277] KEARNS 2011, esp. 738: „The society depicted in the poems is differently organized from that of the archaic and classical periods, which also entails important differences in the practice of religion."

[278] HEATH 2011, 57: „Homeric animals are motivated by similar emotions and casual thoughts as humans. They have the same organs of psychological activity ... Animals are credited with such virtues as bravery (and cowardice), industry and parental devotions. They have wills, can yearn, be eager, experience joy, and be proud or disappointed."

[279] For a detailed discussion see KRAPPE 1941.

[280] Krios is a local Spartan variant of Karnos, the seer, who played an important role in the cult legend of the Karneia (Paus. 3.13.3). In addition, Karnos shows marked similarities with Oxylos, who was equally involved in the return of the Heraclids, became the king of Elis and was also credited with founding the Olympic Games. As the name of Krios clearly implies, these figures were most probably animals and their myths ultimately derive from hunting tales related to them.

[281] KYRIELEIS 2006, 55–61, EKROTH 2012.

own son is the supreme test of fidelity and highly appreciated even if it is not accomplished, while the Greeks dismissed this deed as an act of impiety.[282] I think on the contrary that the best parallel in Greek myth for Abraham sacrificing Isaac would be Agamemnon sacrificing Iphigeneia at Aulis (an episode which also shows that the attitude of Greek gods towards human sacrifice was closely similar to that of biblical Jahwe), and that the parallel drawn between Tantalos and Abraham is much stronger in the Mamre episode (Gen. 18), if we accept the notion that Pelops was originally an animal, offered as a meal for the visiting gods.

That Oinomaos appears in this interpretation as a hunter can hardly be a coincidence and suits very well the hypothesis outlined here. His namesakes, Oinopion and Oineus, are both intimately connected with hunting and hunters: Oineus invites hunters to chase the Calydonian boar and Oinopion makes Orion go hunting on Chios.[283] In accordance with their names, both are closely related to Dionysos, who was the father of Oinopion and master of Oineus,[284] and was clearly described as a hunter himself.[285] Though Oinomaos is referred to as the son of Ares, his name also suggests a connection with Dionysos. The main god of Elis, the region which belonged to the mythical kingdom of Oinomaos, was in fact Dionysos[286] and he was even supposed to have been born at the Alpheios.[287] His connection with wild animals is well-known and he was often linked with youths engaged in hunting.[288] His mythical female followers were always regarded as

---

[282] GROTTANELLI 1984, 854–856 referring to the myth of Lykaon as well. Whether the two tales of serving cooked children to the gods are just doublets, the one modelled simply on the other, or developed independently, is not easy to decide (cf. KIRK 1974, 239–240; BORGEAUD 1979, 50 n. 29 expressing different views on this matter), but I think that the strong and curious similarities cannot be incidental. The similarities and differences were aptly described recently by CLARK 2012, 49–50. For Lykaon see most recently KOSSAIFI 2012.

[283] The similarities between Oinopion and Oinomaos were already noticed by RENAUD 2004, 255–256. For Oinopion see also FONTENROSE 1981, 5–12. Oineus was the son of Agrios and father of Meleagros, both names deriving from hunting: CHANTRAINE 1956, 36–65.

[284] Oinopion: Diod. 5.79.1; Apoll. *Epit.* 1.9; Oineus is even supposed to have been an earlier wine-god (STASINOPOULOU-KAKAROUGA 1997, 919).

[285] Eur. *Bacch.* 135–139; 1146; 1189–1190.

[286] Paus. 6. 26. 1-2.

[287] Hom. hymn cited by Diodor. 3.66.

[288] ISLER-KERÉNYI 2007, 133, 137–139, 155.

wild hunters and his priest in Boiotia performed a ritual chase, where he was armed with a sword and entitled to kill whomever he was able to catch.[289]

Beside the obvious similarities with the myth of Sedna, mentioned above, there is also a detail, which is worth noting in this context, that Sedna's father uses a vehicle, the kanoo, which is normally employed also for hunting. This detail is actually matched by Oinomaos' chariot and strongly suggests that this element is (in contrast to Pelops' chariot) an integral part of the myth, offerring an explanation for the appearance of early chariot representations found at Olympia. The previous interpretations of the helmeted figures standing in chariots and/ or brandishing (a lost) spear as Pelops or as youthful Zeus are therefore to be abandoned. Nor are they heroic warriors participating in some kind of a chariot race or aristocratic dedicators in general, but can be seen as the depictions of the local hero hunter, Oinomaos. Alternatively they might represent the hunters themselves, who visited the sanctuary before and after the actual hunt.[290]

The myth of Pelops and Hippodameia appears therefore at first glance as a simple abduction of a bride, but is primarily concerned with hunting and seems to have been transformed into a bridal race or contest only secondarily. The links with hunting in the sanctuary of Olympia are also numerous and derive from many different sources.

As demonstrated in detail above, the game animals were mainly wild or feral cattle, hunted and considered as high-prestige game animals in all periods of history. And these animals were typically dark colored.[291] This might be the reason for naming the animal as Pelops, in a manner typically used by hunters, since this name can most probably be taken to mean „dark-faced"[292]. The „darkness" of

---

[289] Plut. *Quest. Gr.* 38 (*mor.* 299 E–F). The name of the festival, Agrionia, clearly connects it with the hunt.

[290] The most complete collection of the chariot models and charioteers found in the sanctuary is Heilmeyer 1994. For the interpretation of the early human figures in Olympia in general see HIMMELMANN 2002. It seems to be decisive for the interpretation of these figures that in one case (HEILMEYER 1994, no. 47) there is a dog in the chariot. This animal would be absolutely unnecessary for a chariot race, but is quite logical if we assume a hunt.

[291] VON LENGERKEN 1955, VAN VUURE 2005.

[292] KRETSCHMER 1938, 5 and 1940, 236–237 most recently accepted by ROBERTSON 2010, 74. FRISK 1973, 498 (s.v. pelidnos) is cautious and terms this etymology „ganz unsicher". BEEKES 2010, 1167 (s.v. pelidnos) does not include any reference to Pelops, perhaps for the same reason. CHANTRAINE 1999, 876 added correctly, but clearly rhetorically „mais avec quel sens?", since the explanation given by Kretschmer (light-

Pelops is actually only reflected but not explained by the black ram sacrificed to him (Paus. 5.13.2) and is likely to result from the dark colouring of the specific game animals, which was one of their most important and distinctive features, differentiating them from their domesticated counterparts. It is also remarkable that the heads of the suitors in the myth were used like real aurochs' heads in Çatalhöyük, like horns of consecration on Bronze Age Crete, and like *boukrania* in later Greek sanctuaries.[293] This line of tradition perfectly suits and explains the mythical display of the heads of the suitors.[294] So Pelops is likely to have denoted originally the wild bulls hunted in this region and depicted by the hundreds of miniature figurines found in the sanctuary, where the mistress of the animals, traditionally associated with bulls, was worshipped.[295]

In this way an explanation for connecting the two parts of the myth as well as an overall interpretation of both emerges: the myth of Pelops seems to deal with the hunting of a wild animal of this particular name, which is pursued, killed and afterwards cooked in a cauldron, aiming at or actually effecting its restoration to life.[296] This interpretation means the „chronological" reversal of the two parts of

---

colored indoeuropean newcomers designating the dark-colored original inhabitants of the south in this way) is clearly out of question (although apparently accepted as such by von KAMPTZ 1982, 331). BURKERT 1972, 112 n. 19 thus accepting the etymology attempted to give a symbolic meaning, deriving it from the ritual, which does not seem to be convincing either. It is relevant to remember in this context that the successful suitor of Atalante was according to a widespread version Melanion, with a clearly similar meaning. Cf. FONTENROSE 1981, 176–178. The meaning supposed by DREES 1967, 15 ("der die Fülle erzeugt") seems to be singular and unsubstantiated.

[293] PÖTSCHER 1990, 195–205.

[294] A similar explanation, the poetic anthropomorphisation of apotropaic animal heads (a practice actually observed among different peoples), in order to create a horroristic effect, has already been suggested for the motif in general (GOBRECHT 1996, 262).

[295] For the important role of Artemis in the cult at Olympia see Appendix IX and the section on ritual prescriptions. That the worship of Zeus at Olympia was preceded by the cult of a female deity, is a widespread hypothesis, even if the identity of the goddess is disputed. For the widespread and old association of the great goddess with the bulls (attested e.g. by the monuments Çatalhöyük and minoan Crete) cf. LEHMANN-HARTLEBEN 1939; DIETRICH 1974, 110–117.

[296] HUBBARD 1987, 11 has already suggested quite reasonably that Tantalus actually killed, dismembered and boiled Pelops in the cauldron as an attempt at imparting immortality to him.

the myth,²⁹⁷ as known from the ancient sources, but finds some corroboration in the fact that one of the earlier suitors of Hippodameia was equally called Pelops.²⁹⁸ Moreover, the comparison with Melikertes shows that the chase of the hero child clearly preceded the cooking in the cauldron: as Apollodorus clearly says (3.28), Athamas hunted his son Learkhos as a deer and Ino put Melikertes afterwards in the boiling cauldron. As already noted, it is most reasonable to assume that Athamas killed both children in a similar way and Ino attempted to revive Melikertes, not to kill him.²⁹⁹ So if the chariot race of Pelops really evolved from a chase story, as it most probably did, then it is also likely to have preceeded the resurrection from the boiling cauldron.

Therefore the myth and the ritual may have arisen *pari passu*³⁰⁰ in the following way: as long as hunting was practised intensively, the animals called 'pelopes' were cooked in cauldrons. This praxis involved ritual elements (funeral ceremonies for the dead animals and preservation of their bones intact), aiming at securing the continuity or sustainability of the hunt with an accompanying mythical rationale that the hunter who observes the divine prescriptions will continue to be successful, because the animal will be resurrected by the gods from the cauldron and will therefore be available again the next time. Later on, when hunting was abandoned mainly because the extinction of the game animals, the accompanying rituals were gradually transformed and the myth was also adapted accordingly, to explain the change and the introduction of the newly established rituals, i.e. the athletic and equestrian contests.

Now, it is evident that hunting in general was of primary importance for a very long time in early human history but that it lost this role in real life relatively early, after the adoption of agriculture as the primary means of subsistance. Afterwards,

---

[297] This is also suggested by the Lapp tale quoted in Appendix X. It might be objected that it contradicts Propp's rule concerning the strict and unchanging order of the functions/motifs in the folktales. The rule is, however, not necessarily universal and has been challenged Cf. the relevant passage from the most recent Handbook (KÖHLER-ZÜLCH 2012, 740–741): "Strukturell sind Tötung und W. des Helden nicht handlungsinitiierend, sondern ereignen sich im Laufe und/oder am Schluß der Handlung und präsentieren den Helden in einer außerordentlichen Situation der Hilfsbedürftigkeit."

[298] Schol Pind. Ol. 1.127: Pelops opountios, Opous being possibly a local settlement on the fringes of Elis (Diod. 14.17.8). BUTTERWORTH 1966, 9–10 was also correct in stating that „he (i.e. Pelops) is plainly a composite figure."

[299] PACHE 2004, 148. This view was already expressed by LESKY 1931. More details: HALM-TISSERANT 1993, 180–185.

[300] HARRISON 1927, 16, 327–331; VERSNEL 1993, 74–79.

the hunt of large and dangerous animals played an important role as a privilege of rulers or aristocrats and was retained in various forms of myths and fairy tales. The myth of Pelops may simply be seen in the light of other popular Greek myths originating from paleolithic traditions, which were long obsolete and hardly relevant in historical times.[301] However, as it is intimately linked with Olympia, and because the sanctuary shows clear signs of practising rituals connected with real hunting in the Geometric Age, it is tempting to venture another explanation, i.e. that the hunt reflected by the myth was not the subsistance hunt of paleolithic people, but the pastime of Early Iron Age aristocrats visiting Olympia and its environs for cattle-hunting.

The strongest evidence for this hypothesis comes from the archaeological material, which is abundant in the Geometric Age. The miniature bronze figurines discussed above attest that hunting was practiced here and that the special game animals represented the main attraction of the region, which most probably account for the extraordinary popularity of the sanctuary. The tripod cauldrons, also found in astonishingly great numbers at Olympia[302], fit this hypothesis as well, since they were most probably used for the practical purpose of preparing meat dishes[303] and testify to the importance attached to this type of vessel in the ritual. And since the cauldron plays such a central role in the myth of Pelops, an intimate connection between ritual and myth can be reasonably supposed in the way suggested above.[304] Following the changes of cult practice in the sanctuary, the myth of Pelops was also adjusted: with the gradual disappearance of hunting, the importance of the cauldron story faded out, so too did the practice of dedicating large tripod cauldrons, and the mythical chase was transformed into a contest and served as an aition of the Games.

This interpretation of the myth may explain the otherwise perplexing phenomenon, the strong connection between the cauldron myth and athletic events, and specifically between Pelops and the Olympic Games.[305] It was suggested already in antiquity that the games were celebrated in honour of the dead Pelops, in similar fashion to the games celebrated in honour of the murdered Pelias. But it is plain, how inconsistent the resurrection and the celebration of funeral games

---

[301] BURKERT 1979, 94–97.
[302] MAASS 1978, KIDERLEN 2010.
[303] Cf. above note 46.
[304] For a similar reasoning see SLATER 1989, 495–497.
[305] PACHE 2004, 93: „the connection between the death of the infant Pelops and the establishment of the games is problematic".

actually were: ancient tradition unanimously attests that it was the deceased and not his resurrection from the cauldron which was commemorated by the athletic contests.[306] Modern interpretations faced this problem in two different ways: scholars sought to explain the origins of the athletic events either as emerging from real funeral games celebrated for deceased persons or from initiation rites involving only a mock death and symbolic resurrection.[307] Neither can be regarded as an entirely satisfactory explanation[308]: Funeral games for real personalities were certainly celebrated but never became so popular among different peoples, as those ones for mythical persons which were on the other hand established only in later periods.[309] The initiation paradigm on the other hand, has been rightly challenged recently (partly by its former proponents)[310] and is certainly difficult to apply to the Olympic Games for several reasons: success was promised only for a very few participants, participation could be reiterated several times already in the earliest period, and most importantly, according to the tradition, it was common practice that the participants were first men and that boys were admitted only afterwards. So it is not surprising that both theories, regarded by their proponents as mutually exclusive, were finally rejected altogether.[311] But actually, if adjusted in the sense suggested by the present explanation, I think they can be combined and be seen as partially true: the funeral aspect was really dominant and not merely symbolic, but the dead was instead of a human person a game animal,[312] and there was no initiation of entire age groups, but only hunting, which played an important role in some initiation rites e.g. in Cretan pederasty, referred to above.

---

[306] It is clear that the variant tradition that Pelops instituted the games in honour of the dead Oinomaos or in memory of the earlier suitors was also derived from the same basic idea, i.e. that the institution was to honour the deceased.

[307] For the different theories cf. ULF – WEILER 1980.

[308] Already pointed out by SANSONE 1988, 21–23 and 111–112.

[309] Privately organised funeral games for deceased relatives were typical for the archaic period and attracted competitors from far away, but were once-only celebrations and were not institutionalised. Funeral games organised by political communities for some important citizens, e.g. founders of a city, were recurrent events (mainly annual ones) but did not attract participants from outside or were even restricted to the home of the honoured person. ROLLER 1981.

[310] GRAF 2003. cf. DOWDEN 2011 as well.

[311] WEILER – ULF 1980.

[312] Mourning ceremonies for dead (hunted or sacrificed) animals are widely attested among hunter-gatherers: FRAZER 1911, 223, PAULSON – HULTKRANTZ – JETTMAR 1962, 74–75, 93, 385–386.

Conclusion

According to the hypothesis presented here, wild or feral cattle represented a speciality of the region surrounding Olympia and may explain the early popularity of the sanctuary. The animals were hunted by aristocrats arriving from distant regions of the Peloponnese and following the hunt the same animals were most probably cooked in tripod cauldrons, dedicated and found in great quantities at Olympia. The dedication of small animal figurines made of bronze and terracotta can equally be explained from rituals observed by hunters. This cult practice is absolutely different from the usual sacrifices for the Olympic gods, so often described by the Homeric epic, but is not implausible, since Olympia is conspicuously absent from the epic and also because the miniature animal figurines from geometric Olympia reveal a cult practice, which is fundamentally different from those generally known from epic and later Greek sanctuaries. It is most probably not a mere coincidence that the early cult at Olympia, not mentioned by Homer, seems intimately linked precisely with Artemis, the mistress of wild animals, who is conspicuously under-represented in the epic, but played an especially important role in Olympia.

The Olympic Games, most probably consisting initially in a ritual chase, can be supposed to be part of the ceremony accompanying the common feasts after the successful hunt ("animal ceremonialism"). The rapid growth of votive dedications in the sanctuary during the 8th century BC is most probably due to the intensification of hunting, which inevitably led to the extinction of the wild or feral cattle. Thus hunting, the core of the annual festivals held at the sanctuary, gradually disappeared and was finally abandoned altogether. The first athletic contests, the running events, are likely to have evolved from rituals practised after each successful hunt, and presumably attained greater importance as the hunt became increasingly difficult. Finally, as hunting became impossible, the ceremonies were transformed into running contests, and by adding new athletic disciplines, the games eventually developped into a replacement event for the aristocrats, who visited the sanctuary previously for the sake of hunting.

The mythical tales concerning the cooking and resurrection of Pelops, as well as his contest with Oinomaos, followed the development of the rituals practised in the sanctuary: with the introduction of athletic and equestrian contests the figure of Pelops was anthropomorphised and the story originally related with hunting practices became the aition of the games.

Appendices

I. The Staphylodromia

The name seems to be linguistically clear, but its real meaning is rather obscure. Usually it is assumed that bunches of grapes were given to the runners chasing the selected forerunner, but the fruit was also supposed to be carried by the forerunner.[313] While these propositions are not impossible, they do not seem very convincing. Apart from the fact that it is quite difficult to run with a bunch of grapes in one hand and to catch the forerunner (presumably with the other one), grapes are quite surprising in the context of a festival dedicated to Apollo. It is also true that generally no kind of fruit is carried by runners and in Greece there are no parallels in this respect either. Moreover, grapes were not necessarily ripe at the time of the festival, the main vintage period being generally later[314] and it is absolutely unexplained why the runners would have carried the bunches. So it is perhaps not surprising to find that another suggestion has already been made, which denies the literal meaning of *staphyle* and tries to find another, symbolic one.[315] I must confess that I am not convinced that this novel explanation would be closer to the ancient intentions than the usual one.

One can observe, however, that because grapes were generally known and had a typical form, the name could be used to denote objects with a similar shape[316] and these parallels clearly show that σταφύλη not only means the bunch, but the single berries as well. While it is much easier to carry a single berry of grape than a whole bunch in our hands while running, this does not explain the reason why such grapes were probably necessary for the running or why this kind of fruit would have been appropriate to the festival. So I would suggest that the σταφύλη was a substitute for a wild berry, the cornelian cherry, which has roughly the same shape and is by its very name (κράνεια) closely connected to the Karneia. As Pausanias (3.13. 5) reports

---

[313] SCANLON 2002, 150.
[314] Already observed by BURKERT 1977, 356–357.
[315] ROBERTSON 2003, 62–63.
[316] σταφύλη is also used for the plummet of a level and in an anatomical sense (uvula) and gave the name to the bladder-nut (staphylodendron in Plin. *Nat.Hist.* 16.69).

"There is also another account of the name; in Trojan Ida there grew in a grove of Apollo cornel-trees, which the Greeks cut down to make the Wooden Horse. Learning that the god was wroth with them they propitiated him with sacrifices and named Apollo Carneus from the cornel-tree, a custom prevalent in the olden time making them transpose the r and the a." (English Translation by W. H. S. Jones and H. A. Ormerod)[317]

The fruit of this plant was not necessarily ripe at the time of the festival, but this was irrelevant, because the running was certainly not concerned with harvesting this fruit (as it was evidently not concerned with vintage either). It was a chase, where the forerunner had to be reached. How this actually happened and how it was controlled, we do not know, but a few pieces of cornelian cherry in the hands of the runners would certainly make sense, because in this way they were able to prove beyond doubt, simply by the red colour of the berries appearing on the skin of the forerunner, that they had reached and touched him. This suggestion cannot be proven in any way, but is certainly attractive for another reason as well. If this scenario is accepted, the red colour of the taint appearing on the skin of the forerunner can easily be seen as a substitute for blood and is therefore in perfect harmony with the general impression that the chase was a symbolic hunt.

Usually, however, the staphylodromia is usually interpreted as „a harvest festival"[318] or as „a vegetation ritual, performed in order to affect the harvest, notably the grape harvest". [319] The various parallels, which were repeatedly adduced to underpin this interpretation, fall in two categories: Most often it is

---

[317] Of course, it is by no means granted that the connection of Apollo Karneios with the cornel tree is etymologically correct (most probably it is not cf. above note 31), but the explanation shows that a connection between the plant and the god's festival was contemplated and that this was not necessarily due to the similarity of the words Karneios and Kraneia, since in this case a series of other words or folk-etymologies (starting e.g. from κρανίον or κράνος) could have occurred.

[318] SCANLON 2002, 31.

[319] PETTERSSON 1992, 68 with references in his note 401. Pettersson himself offers a different interpretation, connecting the staphylodromia with initiation and with divination: „the pursued man was a seer, and the catching of him symbolized the possibility of a renewal of the relations between men and gods, as if there were a contract which had to be renewed at regular intervals." (ibid. 72) The suggestion seems hardly any more convincing than the traditional reading of the festival.

the Athenian *oschophoria*, which is mentioned, but ethnographic parallels from Europe are also cited in this connection.

Admittedly, in the *oschophoria*, the grape also plays an important role and there is also some kind of running contest, but the two seem to be unconnected within the festival: the grape branches are carried in a procession accompanied by songs and the running is a separate event. The date of the festival is also considerably different, since it belongs to late autumn and not to the high summer. It is usually interpreted as a vintage festival, but most recently and probably correctly, this connection is denied and the festival is seen as a social event with some initiatory character.[320] The Karneia was interpreted in a similar fashion, but even if this were true, the similarities between the two festivals are rather superficial.

The ethnographic parallels from northern Europe can be regarded in contrast as closer parallels; it is only the interpretation of the similarities which should be corrected. Mannhardt collected several customs, where peasants believed in a certain kind of grain spirit, imagined as some kind of animal (most often a ram) which was chased and killed after completing the harvest.[321] These examples were used afterwards by Wide to demonstrate that the Karneia originated from a similar harvest or rather vintage ceremony.[322] The similarity of these rituals to the Karneia cannot be denied, but there is a basic difference: in all the adduced parallels, the ram or the animals used in a similar way are seen as the spirit of the grain and are chased immediately after the harvest, but there is nothing in the Karneia, which would suggest that it occurred immediately after the harvest or that it had any connection with harvesting grain. It is only the grapes of the staphylodomoi which can be used to suggest some kind of vintage, but the timing of the festival actually prevents us from connecting it with the conclusion of this agricultural activity. So even though the ceremony, i.e. the ritual chase, is obviously similar to that of the staphylodromia, this similarity cannot be explained by reducing the staphylodromia to a harvest festival.

As the Dorians practising the Karneia and the peoples of northern Europe surely did not stand in direct or indirect contact with each other, it is very likely that the similar ritual originated from some prehistoric and widespread custom, which was not restricted to ethnic, social or other groups, however loosely they are defined. Supposing that this custom was originally connected with grain-

---

[320] PARKER 2007, 211–217.
[321] MANNHARDT 1877, 155–183.
[322] WIDE 1893, 75–81.

spirits or harvest ceremonies, it is hard to see, why this ceremony should have disappeared in so many agrarian groups of people and should be practised only by the Dorians – and moreover in a form which actually does not show any connection with the supposedly original context of harvesting grain. So it is more likely that the connection with the grain harvest is only a secondary one and that it is the Karneia which is closer to the original form and function of the ritual than the more recent northern harvest customs.

Since in the case of the Karneia, we not only have the description of the ceremony/ritual but also the related mythical rationale, it is appropriate to consider this evidence as well. It is not surprising that the myths concerning Karnos do not show any connection with harvesting grain. Instead they concentrate on the mythical wanderings of the ancestors of the Dorians. Pausanias (3.13.3-4) relates two different versions, which are both worth citing:

> *"Carneus, whom they surname "of the House," had honors in Sparta even before the return of the Heracleidae, his seat being in the house of a seer, Crius (Ram) the son of Theocles. The daughter of this Crius was met as she was filling her pitcher by spies of the Dorians, who entered into conversation with her, visited Crius and learned from him how to capture Sparta.*
>
> *The cult of Apollo Carneus has been established among all the Dorians ever since Carnus, an Acarnanian by birth, who was a seer of Apollo. When he was killed by Hippotes the son of Phylas, the wrath of Apollo fell upon the camp of the Dorians. Hippotes went into banishment because of the bloodguilt, and from this time the custom was established among the Dorians of propitiating the Acarnanian seer. But this Carnus is not the Lacedaemonian Carneus of the House, who was worshipped in the house of Crius the seer while the Achaeans were still in possession of Sparta."* (English Translation by W.H.S. Jones, and H.A. Ormerod)

The story of Karnos is narrated in more detail by Apollodorus (*Bibl.* 2. 169–180). He omits the local Spartan version about Krios leading the Dorians into their new home, but introduces after the assassination of Karnos (whom he does not mention by name) another seer, Oxylos, who is an even more treacherous leader of the Dorians than Krios, because he deceives not the enemy, but the

Dorians themselves. The main common function of all these mythical figures is that they lead the Dorians into their new home. In addition, as the name of Krios shows beyond reasonable doubt, this leading figure was imagined as an animal, the ram.

Animals leading the ancestors of whole peoples into their new home are known from various legends[323] and it is only to be assumed that such a legend formed the basis of the Karneia as well, which remained the main festival celebrating the Dorian migration. The animal was sometimes a wild one being chased and not reached by the mythical hunters, or a tame one, which was observed and eventually sacrificed by the people seeking their new home. It seems quite reasonable to assume that the second version is just an updated version of the first, since the magical game animal is replaced by a domesticated one, which however has never been used by humans.

The *staphylodromia*, where a runner representing this special animal was chased, is connected to a myth in which the leading animal is already anthropomorphized. The ritual can thus reasonably be interpreted as a ritualized hunt, representing the mythical wanderings of the Dorians. It was not just „a conspicuous element of the Karneia"[324], but most probably its most important central part. The importance of the leading animal or person is clearly attested by the alternative name of the festival, *agetoria*. The ritual chase and the myth of the wandering peoples is not primarily related to agricultural activities, but constitutes the hunters' or pastoralists' legacy and is therefore conserved only sporadically under special circumstances which are far from each other both in space and time.

---

[323] KRAPPE 1942. The most well-known examples from classical antiquity are Kadmos and Aeneas (following and observing a cow and a sow respectively), but Boiai on the Peloponnese had a similar foundation legend involving a hare (Paus. 3.22.12). The Hungarian legend about Hunor and Magor is about following a miraculous deer, which finally disappears, like the hare in the previous legend. The appearance of a miraculous deer persisted as a motif in the legends of later centuries as well: C. Pschmadt, *Die Sage von der verfolgten Hinde. Ihre Heimat und Wanderung, Bedeutung und Entwicklung mit besonderer Berücksichtigung ihrer Verwendung in der Literatur des Mittelalters*, Diss. Greifswald 1911 (non vidi).

[324] PETTERSSON 1992, 68.

II. Greek Geometric Bull Figurines Outside Olympia, the Kabeirion and Crete

The following list is arranged according to the provenance of the pieces and can certainly not pretend to be exhaustive, but I think it can be regarded as representative:
- Athens Acropolis: 2 bulls/oxen[325]
- Bassae: 1 bovid[326]
- Delphi: 13 bulls/bovines[327]
- Sanctuary of the Dioskuroi-Kabeiroi near Chalkis: 13 pieces[328]
- Lousoi: 2 bulls now in Karlsruhe F 1931, 1932[329]
- Mila in Messenia: 3 bovids[330]
- Tegea: 6 reclining oxen[331]

In addition, there are some pieces with unknown provenance, which are probably originating from Olympia (*Fig. 5*):
- Athens, Benaki Museum 29935 (bull from the Peloponnese)[332]
- Boston, Museum of Fine Arts 67.282 (bull, aquired in Greece)
  64.1461 (bovine with long horns, presumably bull)[333]
  2001.167 (bull)
- Baltimore, Walters Art Mus. 54.2379: one bull most probably from Olympia[334]
- Budapest, Mus. Fine Arts 51.946: unpublished, said to come from the Peloponnese
- Univ. Missouri-Columbia MAA 86.80: one bull, said to come from Olympia[335]

---

[325] DE RIDDER 1896, 187 nos. 513–514.
[326] PAPATHANASOPOULOS 1969, 148 Nr. 25 Pl. 147 g.
[327] ROLLEY 1969, 76–79 Nos. 99–108, 110–112, Pl. XIX–XX.
[328] PAPAVASILEIOU 1912, 145–153, figs.3–6.
[329] VOYATZIS 1990, 144, 278 L 11–12, fig. 26, pl. 81.
[330] KARAGIORGIA 1972, 18–19, Pl. 21 γ, δ, ε.
[331] DUGAS 1921, 342–344 Fig. 2; VOYATZIS 1990, 144–147, B34–37; pl. 78–80.
[332] ATHANASSOPOULOU *et al.* 2003, 190 Cat. no. 121.
[333] COMSTOCK – VERMEULE 1971, 19 Nos. 17, 18.
[334] HILL 1955, 41 Pl. 30, Fig. 10.
[335] LANGDON 1987, 58–61 Figs. 4–6; LANGDON 1993, 55–57, No. 6.

*Fig. 5. Geometric bovine figurines from Greece
(Baltimore, Walters Art Gallery; New York, Metropolitan Museum)*

- Kansas, Nelson-Atkins Mus. 34.288 and 33.1520: two unpublished bulls
- New York, Metropolitan Museum of Art 1972.118.82: one bull „said to have been found at Olympia"[336]

These are not more than 50 pieces altogether, even if the pieces with unknown provenance are counted. Numbers are not given for geometric bovids at the Amyklaion[337] and Rhodos at the sanctuary of Zeus Atabyrios.[338] Compared with the ca. 2500 pieces from Olympia, Crete and the Kabeirion, these numbers are really negligable.

---

[336] VON BOTHMER 1950, no. 34.
[337] TSOUNTAS 1892, 12.
[338] HEILMEYER 1979, 32–33.

III. Biological and Ethological Characteristics of Wild and Feral Bovines

The basic facts about the species are collected and thoroughly discussed in the recent monograph by Van Vuure. The brief summaries of some chapters are quoted here with minor omissions.

„In 1758, Linnaeus gave the scientific name Bos taurus to the domestic derivative of the aurochs; the latter one got the name Bos primigenius from Bojanus in 1827. The aurochs probably emerged as a species between 1.5 and 2 million years ago in India, in a period in which the global grass area expanded greatly. From India, the aurochs spread to other parts of Asia, Europe and Africa. It inhabited mainly temperate and subtropical zones. Though the relationships between the different species of the Bovini tribe have not been explained completely as yet, the aurochs is probably most related to the gaur and the banteng" but caffer and bison are also close relatives and were sometimes confused with aurochs.[339]

„One aspect of the aurochs that has long been a focus of interest and a subject of discussion is its size. Early descriptions give only vague indications about this. Numerous aurochs bones have survived, even a number of almost complete skeletons. Since the dimensions of these bones are well known, it has proved possible to reconstruct the original size of the animal from them. ... Their withers varied between 160 and 180 cm for the (Holocene) aurochs bull, and to have been around 150 cm for the (Holocene) aurochs cow. For the Pleistocene aurochs the height of the withers was probably well over 10 cm greater."[340]

„The numerous aurochs skulls with horn cores, and a limited number of keratin horns, show that the horns of this animal had a characteristic shape and position. This typical shape and position may be found throughout the distribution area, which shows it to have been very stable. The horns were pointed forward and curved inward."[341]

„Another feature of aurochs horns is their characteristic position, which determines their 'forwardness'. On the basis of five skulls, Ewald & Laurer (1911) determined the angle of the horn cores in relation to the surface of the head. This angle varied between 50 and 60 degrees. For the Russian distribution area, Gromova (1931) determined an average angle of 63 degrees. Mensuration of

---

[339] VAN VUURE 2005, 40.
[340] VAN VUURE 2005, 119–120.
[341] VAN VUURE 2005, 135.

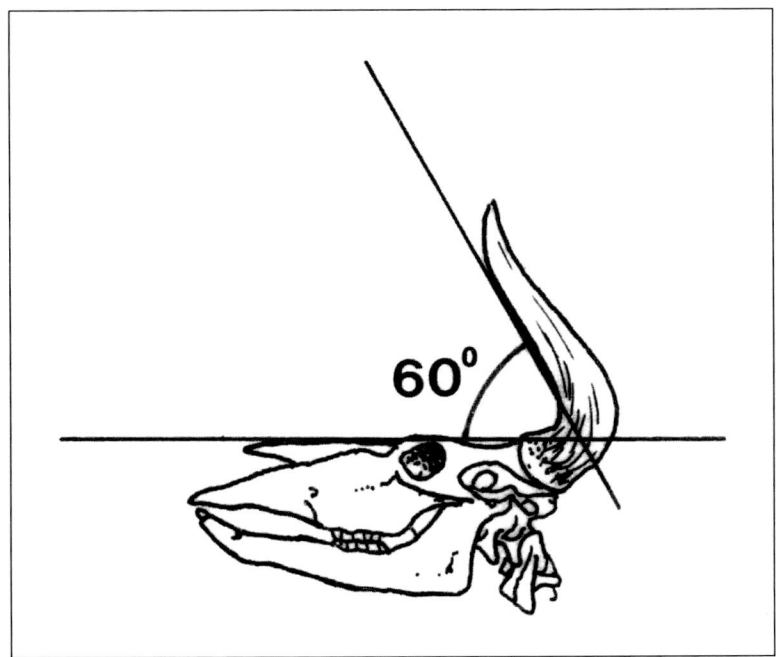

Fig. 6. The characteristic position of aurochs horns (after VAN VUURE 2005, fig. 26)

six aurochs skulls at the Natuurhistorisch Museum Naturalis in Leiden (author's observation) revealed that this angle varied between 50 and 70 degrees, with an average of 59 degrees."[342] (*Fig. 6*)

„On the basis of paintings from caves (those of Lascaux, for example) and pictures from the 16th century (including that of the 'Augsburg aurochs'), combined with early descriptions of the aurochs, contemporary genetic studies and comparisons with wild cattle species that still exist, it has proved possible to draw a relatively clear image of the fur colour of the aurochs. There was a clear difference between the colour of the cow and that of the bull. The bull was blackish brown to black, with a narrow, lighter stripe (eelstripe) on the back. The cow was reddish brown, like the calf."[343]

„Probably around 7000 BC., the aurochs was turned into a domestic animal ('domesticated') in the Middle East. Domestication could secure a more stable

---

[342] VAN VUURE 2005, 131–132.
[343] VAN VUURE 2005, 155.

Fig. 7. Comparison of aurochs and domestic cattle (after VAN VUURE 2005, fig. 16)

source of food than hunting. As a result of domestication, as well as intentional and unintentional selection, the external and internal characteristics of the aurochs changed into those of the hundreds of cattle breeds that were produced by these processes. The variations in body size, fur colour, horn shape and udder size increased. The differences between cows and bulls (sexual dimorphism) decreased."[344]

„Domestication also resulted in a shortening and narrowing (relatively speaking: a broadening) of the skull all kinds of new horn shapes developed. Increasingly, the original aurochs horn shape receded into the background. Instead of their original forward and inward position, the horns started to point upward, outward and backward. Hornless-ness was no longer prey to natural selection and occurred more and more frequently."[345]

The main differences compared to the domesticated cattle are best illustrated in *Fig. 7*.

---

[344] VAN VUURE 2005, 174.
[345] VAN VUURE 2005, 170–171.

„Roughly speaking, the European bison inhabited the drier forest types in the lowlands and the higher mountains areas, while the aurochs frequented the wetter forest types in the lowlands and the lower mountain areas. ... The aurochs is likely to have distinguished between its summer and its winter habitat. In summer, the emphasis may have been on grasses and graminoids in the wetter habitats; in winter, on bark, branches, tree leaves and bushes, as well as any edible remains of grasses and forbs in the drier, wooded habitats. Depending on the vegetation, the winter temperature, the geographical situation and the density of the population, the contrast between the summer and winter habitat will probably have been more or less marked."[346]

„The aurochs' preference for river valleys as a summer habitat is still reflected in that of its domesticated descendants. During the growing season, present-day domestic cattle also prefer to live in riverside grasslands. The presence of water and the attractive food have been shown to be the main reasons for this preference."[347]

„The habitat of the aurochs must have been situated in a landscape that consisted of extensive forests alternated by several types of marshes. Bone finds and old descriptions suggest that there was a strong affinity between the aurochs and marshes and marshy forests, to which it owed its nickname 'marsh walker'. River valleys, coastal salt marshes and other types of marshes are likely to have been among the aurochs' favourite areas."[348]

„The information obtained from early descriptions and through comparison with wild cattle species still in existence suggests that the social structure among aurochs was similar to that of related bovine species. This social structure consisted of mixed groups of cows, calves and young bulls beside smaller groups of older bulls and single old bulls. The mating season and, consequently, also the season in which calves were born, were limited to certain periods of the year. The rutting season in Poland was in late summer (presumably August, September); calves were born in late spring (presumably May, June). Just before and during the mating season, the grown bulls would go to the mixed groups to mate with the cows there."[349]

---

[346] VAN VUURE 2005, 249–250.
[347] VAN VUURE 2005, 254.
[348] VAN VUURE 2005, 259.
[349] VAN VUURE 2005, 271.

IV. Aurochs and Wild Cattle in the Ancient Mediterranean

The earliest relevant finds come from the prehistoric settlement of Çatalhöyük in the southern part of Anatolia, in the Konya plain (*Fig. 8*). Excavations revealed here a large number of shrines with remarkably rich decoration from the 7th and 6th millenia BC, which certainly attest the paramount importance of wild animals and especially cattle in the religious practices.[350] The rich environment provided ideal living conditions for wild cattle and the earliest evidence for their domestication also comes from this region. Although the shrines were all decorated by aurochs horns, the analysis of the osteological material revealed that hunting played a relatively small role in subsistence at Çatalhöyük: the faunal remains are in fact mainly sheep/goat, with cattle forming only about 20 percent.[351] Cattle's symbolic value was thus not tied to their subsistence role, which was always minor in the Near East, but more likely to their power and danger. They seem to have been the high-prestige game species and became therefore the central elements of feasts as sacrificial animals.[352]

Fig. 8. Interior of building VI.A.8 from Catalhöyük (after MELLAART 1967, fig. 42)

---

[350] In general see e.g. MELLAART 1967; RICE 1988, 72–84.
[351] RUSSELL – MARTIN 2005.
[352] RUSSELL 2012, 18–19.

In Egypt the aurochs was regularly hunted and used in the earliest dynastic period as a symbolic representation of the pharaoh as well, but later on seems to become extinct. III Amenhotep (1413–1377) left a remarkable hunting story inscribed on a scarab: an aurochs herd of 176 heads was suddenly found in the Nile delta and was reported to the pharaoh, who immediately travelled there and killed 75 of the animals. II Ramses (1301–1234) is depicted while hunting an aurochs, but the scene depicts not his homeland but some region in northern Mesopotamia.[353] There is however a great deal of representation of feral cattle, which were hunted and caught alive in order to be sacrificed. „On the basis of the colour and the shape of the horns, it seems logical to conclude that the wild cattle in question were actually domesticated animals, which either went wild entirely (for which theory there are many indications) or which may have been kept inside cattle grids for religious purposes, to be caught or killed. Some of the bovine animals depicted were caught alive. ... It seems likely that initially, these were wild aurochs, from which the custom was later transferred to animals gone wild or kept in a feral state."[354]

The presence of aurochs in Bronze Age Anatolia and the Levant is attested by some unambiguous depictions (*Fig. 9*), a relief from Alaca Höyük and a gold vessel from Ras Shamra (Ugarit).[355]

The two famous gold cups from a Mycenean tomb at Vaphio show the capturing of bulls with nets around 1500 BC. Although they were found on the

Fig. 9. Golden wessel from Ugarit and stone relief from Alaca Höyük (after VON LENGERKEN 1955, figs. 93, 100)

---

[353] VON LENGERKEN 1955, 96–110.
[354] VAN VUURE 2005, 139.
[355] VON LENGERKEN 1955, 68, 73–74.

Peloponnese, the cups were most probably manufactured by Cretan goldsmiths and it is likely that the animals were actually captured for the ritual bull-leaping shown on famous and roughly contemporary mural paintings. These depictions show animals with spotted, multicoloured hides, indicating therefore that they are domesticated ones. So the bulls on the Vaphio cups are also likely to have been feral cattle and not genuine wild bulls or aurochs. Osteological evidence, however, shows that aurochs was living on the island during the Bronze Age.[356] When it became extinct we do not know, but the bronze figurines from Kato Syme strongly suggest that it was still hunted in the mountains of the island during the Geometric Age.

A gaming box from Cyprus from the end of the Bronze Age (12th century BC) shows hunting from a chariot, where all the animals flee and only the aurochs bull is turning back or attacking the hunter. (*Fig. 10*)[357]

During the Early Iron Age, the aurochs seems to have been still available in the Near East (*Fig. 11*), but due to hunting, which was presumably a royal privilege, it soon became extinct. Assurnasirpal II (883–859 BC) was able to catch 50 aurochs on a single hunt near the Euphrates and boasted of having killed some 257 aurochs in another list. (*Fig. 12*) He also founded a royal hunting reserve in Assur where aurochs were kept as well. Sancherib (704–681 BC) likewise still hunted 'wild cattle' in Northern Mesopotamia, but there is no information about later hunts in these regions.[358]

Aurochs seems to have become extinct during the early archaic period in Greece. The numerous geometric depictions disappear and wild cattle are nearly absent from the literary evidence as well.

On Crete, we have some depictions strongly reminiscent of aurochs (*Fig. 13*), but these do not necessarily attest the presence of these animals, since the reliefs show clear oriental influences and might be manufactured by artists coming from the Levant or by Greeks under strong Levantine influence.

There is a sarcophagus relief from Cyprus (Golgoi) showing two warriors killing a rather small bull (*Fig. 14*). The context is hunting, but the unique

---

[356] PILALI 1985, 124 with references; NOBIS 1996. VAN VUURE 2005, 51 denies the possibility of an aurochs population on Crete, but he apparently is not aware of the finds attesting the contrary. To be fair, it must be admitted that the osteological evidence does not show that the aurochs population on the island was an indigenous one; it is equally possible that the species was introduced artificially by man during the Bronze Age.
[357] ARUZ 2008, 412–413 (no. 265).
[358] VON LENGERKEN 1955, 60 and 111.

Fig. 10. Late Cypriot ivory gaming box from Enkomi (tomb no. 58). ca. 1250–1050 BC.; London BM GR 1897.0401.996. © Trustees of the British Museum

Fig. 11. Stone reliefs from Zincirli and Tell Halaf (after VON LENGERKEN 1955, figs. 95, 97)

Fig. 12. Relief from the North West Palace at Nimrud (Kalhu). Royal bull hunt of Ashurnasirpal II (875–860 BC). London BM 124532. © Trustees of the British Museum

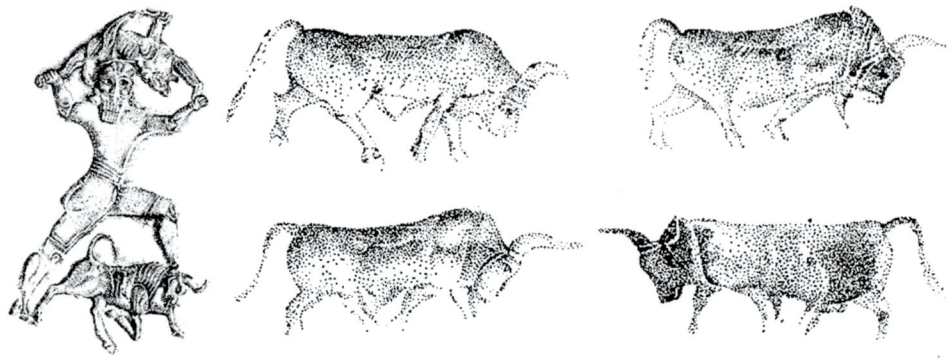

Fig. 13. Bronze reliefs from the Idaean Cave (Crete) (after VON LENGERKEN 1955, figs. 111–112.)

Fig. 14. Sarcophagus relief from Golgoi (Cyprus). ca. 475–450 BC. New York, Metropolitan Museum 74.51.2451.

representation is not likely to depict reality based on autopsy, since the animal is unrealistically small.

That wild cattle were practically extinct by the late archaic period in the southern parts of mainland Greece, is clearly attested by Herodotus (7. 126), who reports at the same time that the horns were highly valued and imported from Thrace:

"In these parts there are many lions and wild oxen (βόες ἄγριοι), whose horns are those very long ones which are brought into Hellas." (English translation by A. D. Godley)

Fig. 15. Wild bull dragged to a ship. Detail of the late Roman mosaic floor of the villa at Piazza Armerina. (© José Luiz Bernardes Ribeiro / Wikimedia commons / CC-BY-SA-4.0)

Whether the expression denotes aurochs or bisons cannot be decided with absolute certainty, because the latter were occasionally described by the same words (*Arist. Mir.* 842b33) and were known and valued as exotic animals by Greeks and Romans alike.[359] But since bisons have not large horns, so the passage is likely to refer to the aurochs. Animals described as βόες ἄγριοι in areas remote from the Mediterranean are likely to denote some other bovine species, e.g. buffalo, gnu or the gaur in Asia and in Africa.[360] Such an exotic animal is shown on the mosaic pavement of the villa at Piazza Armerina (*Fig. 15*)

In his *Bellum Gallicum* (6.28), Julius Caesar called the aurochs by the appropriate Celtic word 'urus', and although his description was judged as not

---

[359] E.g. Paus. 10.13. 1-4; Martialis *epigr*. 1.104.8. KELLER 1887, 53–57.
[360] Aristot. *Hist. Anim.* 499a.4 (βόες οἱ ἄγριοι in Arachosia); Philostr. *Vita Apoll.* 6.24 (βόαγροι in Ethiopia), Strab. 16.4.9 (πλῆθος τῶν ἀγρίων βοῶν also in Ethiopia) cf. KELLER 1887, 61–62.

entirely realistic, it certainly shows the high esteem and prestige attached to these animals:

> *Tertium est genus eorum qui uri appellantur. hi sunt magnitudine paulo infra elephantos, specie et colore et figura tauri. magna vis eorum est et magna velocitas; neque homini neque ferae, quam conspexerunt, parcunt. hos studiose foveis captos interficiunt. hoc se labore durant adulescentes atque hoc genere venationis exercent, et qui plurimos ex his interfecerunt, relatis in publicum cornibus, quae sint testimonio, magnam ferunt laudem. sed adsuescere ad homines et mansuefieri ne parvuli quidem excepti possunt. amplitudo cornuum et figura et species multum a nostrorum boum cornibus differt. haec studiose conquisita ab labris argento circumcludunt atque in amplissimis epulis pro poculis utuntur.*

„There is a third kind, consisting of those animals which are called uri. These are a little below the elephant in size, and of the appearance, color, and shape of a bull. Their strength and speed are extraordinary; they spare neither man nor wild beast which they have espied. These the Germans take with much pains in pits and kill them. The young men harden themselves with this exercise, and practice themselves in this kind of hunting, and those who have slain the greatest number of them, having produced the horns in public, to serve as evidence, receive great praise. But not even when taken very young can they be rendered familiar to men and tamed. The size, shape, and appearance of their horns differ much from the horns of our oxen. These they anxiously seek after, and bind at the tips with silver, and use as cups at their most sumptuous entertainments." (English transl. by W. A. McDevitte and W. S. Bohn)

From ca. the same period the uri are mentioned twice by Vergil in Italy, but these poetic passages (*Georgica* 2.374; 3.532) cannot prove beyond doubt that real aurochs existed in the Po Valley. During the time of the Roman Empire (up to circa 400 AD), many wild animals, including aurochs as well, were caught on a regular basis from around the empire and transported to Rome or other towns to be used in arena fights, as attested by Pliny (*Nat. Hist.* 8.38):

Ceterorum animalium, quae modo convecta undique Italia<e> contigere saepius, formas nihil attinet scrupulose referre. paucissima Scythia gignit inopia fruticum, pauca contermina illi Germania, insignia tamen boum ferorum genera, iubatos bisontes excellentique et vi et velocitate u<r>os, quibus inperitum volgus bubalorum nomen inponit, cum id gignat Africa vituli potius cervique quadam similitudine.

"As to the other animals, which have been of late repeatedly brought to Italy from all parts of the world, it is quite unnecessary to give any minute account of their form. Scythia produces but very few animals, in consequence of the scarcity of shrubs. Germany, which lies close adjoining it, has not many animals, though it has some very fine kinds of wild oxen: the bison, which has a mane, and the urus, possessed of remarkable strength and swiftness. To these, the vulgar, in their ignorance, have given the name of bubalus whereas, that animal is really produced in Africa, and rather bears a resemblance to the calf and the stag." (English transl. by John Bostock)

V. The Extinction of the Aurochs in Europe

Table 1 adapted from VAN VUURE 2005, p. 64 Table 2

Area	Time of disappearance
England	ca. 1300 BC
Italy	1st century BC
Netherlands	ca. 400
Central Europe	ca. 13th century
East Prussia	ca. 1500
Poland	1627

The circumstances of the extinction in Poland are relatively well-documented and studied. It was only in the duchy of Masovia (around Warsaw) where the species is known to have lived free. „From an animal that could initially be hunted freely, it became more rare and the hunt for it increasingly became the privilege of the nobility. In written records of such privileges the aurochs holds a special place among the various types of game. …

A noble privilege of this kind has been passed down from as early as 1298, when Boleslaw, duke of Masovia, granted several villages with grounds in the district of Plock to one knight, Paulecz, reserving, however the hunt for the aurochs in those areas for himself. In 1359, Siemowit IV, duke of Masovia, allows the duchess of Wyszogród to hunt on his entire territory, excluding the hunt for aurochs. Another document of the same tenor is known from 1383. The animal may still have occurred in the east of Masovia around 1436, but its occurrence was gradually restricted more and more to an area southwest of Warsaw, where there were large forests and where an aurochs population could still survive due to protective measures.

The area in question was a forest area of roughly 25,000 ha, divided into several smaller forests, administratively speaking. The complex included the Forest of Bolemów (circa 6000 ha), the Forest of Jaktorów (circa 5900 ha) and the Forest of Wiskitki (circa 13.600 ha).

In the early 15th century, the Polish king Jagiello was still invited by the duke of Masovia, who owned the forests at the time, to hunt for aurochs there. In 1476, however, management of the forests reverted to the Crown; at the same time, the Royal Family came into possession of one of the two last wild aurochs populations. This population was to remain and exist there for another 150 years. The very last wild aurochs population must have occurred in the Polish Royal Forests into the early 16th century. At that time the animals still roamed the entire forest area, but in the second half of the 16th century they occurred exclusively in the Forests of Wiskitki and Jaktorów. Documents concerning these animals, from 1602, 1620 and 1630, only refer to the latter forest.

The organisation of the management of the aurochs population in these areas goes back to the 13th century, at which time there was already a well-organized gamekeeping service, in those days under ducal authority. In 1476 this reverted to the Crown, together with the Royal Forests. The gamekeeping service employed several so-called 'hunters', who played an important role in the aurochs management. Their most important task was to '...keep an eye on the aurochs, let them graze, collect the hay from Jaktorów from the subjects, to supply the aurochs with this in winter, to know the number of animals and give a report to the district manager or the tenant every three months'."[361]

Due to this regulation, the numbers of animals are known fairly accurately and even the composition of the herds is attested during the last ca. 50 years of their existence. The figures recorded relate only to the aurochs population of a relatively small territory (59 km²) at the Forest of Jaktorow. (*Fig. 16*)

Fig. 16. The decline of the last aurochs population in the forests of Jaktorow, Poland (after VAN VUURE 2005, fig. 11)

---

[361] VAN VUURE 2005, 65–71.

Some aurochs were held in captivity in a zoo and possibly survived a few more years, but not much longer.

This well-documented case clearly shows two phenomena: 1) that an aurochs population could survive even on a relatively small, restricted area (250 km^2) for a considerable period, i.e. for centuries after the species became extinct elsewhere; 2) that extinction was, despite protective regulations, inevitable in a few decades after the number of animals fell below a certain threshold.

VI. The Camargue Horses and Bulls

The Camargue denotes the region of the Rhône delta; its climate and environment cannot have differed substantially from the marshy wetlands surrounding Olympia and the lower course of the Alpheios. The Camargue is today, and has been at least for centuries, the home of special feral horses and bulls.

The horses are a small riding horse, born coloured but rapidly turning white with age. „When they reach between 3 and 8 years, they are all white haired and black skinned. This is a consequence of the loss, with age, of pigmentation in the hair; it is controlled genetically ... and is unusual in horses. The only other well-known case was described by Herodotus two millenia ago – the „all white" feral of wild horses of the Pripet (Polesye) Marshes in central Europe – and they also lived in wetlands. ... Camargue horses are hardy and can live and breed on poor forage. They become docile when handled young, but some, lacking application and aptitude, are difficult to train. Their gaits ar often rough and uncomfortable, which is not surprising in view of their conformation. ...

The uncertainty about the origins of modern horses in general has not discouraged several authors from being dogmatic about the origins of the Camargue breed; the several hypotheses... boil down to two main ones, which propose on the one hand a prehistoric origin and on the other an escapee origin.

The first historical record referring to horses in the Camargue region is Phoenician and it mentions wild horses living on the sparse pastures on the edge of the Rhône and records that the horses were hunted for meat by the inhabitants of the delta. The horses may have been wild descendants of the Equus ferus gallicus, but the possibility that they were already escapee domestic animals cannot be excluded. Horses had been domesticated some 1500 years before, and there is no evidence for the presence of any wild populations in southern Europe after 5000 B.C.

The prehistoric hypothesis, which holds that the horses found in the Camargue in the 19th century were a survival of the Magdalenien Equus ferus gallicus, is clearly false in its extreme forms. ... Camargue horses of today are therefore principally or totally of domestic origin."[362]

The origin of the Camargue cattle is equally unclear. „It has either existed from the Middle Ages onward, or the population that lived there in the early 19th century was obliterated by a disease and replaced by a different cattle breed, the

---

[362] DUNCAN 1992, 210–212.

Salers. It lives in a feral state and is used for bullfights. The colour of both sexes is black or blackish brown. The height at the withers is 130 cm in bulls and 120 cm in cows. The curved horns are positioned high. The udder is small."[363]

---

[363] VAN VUURE 2005, 328.

VII. Basic Features of Hunting

Hunting is a well-known kind of human activity, which has been described and analysed in various ways. Because it is of central importance to the present subject and because its complexity is not always realized, a short summary is provided here based on an recent study.

„Certainly by the advent of anatomically modern humans, meat had become a regular component of the diet, to a greater or lesser degree. Before animal domestication, anatomically modern humans acquired most of their meat by hunting. Even after domestication, hunting continued and continues to be practiced in virtually all societies. Even after domestication, hunting continued and continues to be practiced in virtually all societies. Hunting is about more than simply acquiring food.

Hunting and meat tend in all cultures to be valued far beyond their actual contribution to the diet and the prestige accorded to hunters is quite out of proportion to the protein and calories that they provide. ... This prestige is attached primarily to hunting larger mammals, but sometimes extends to the killing of large aquatic turtles and pelagic fish such as tuna. These exceptions seem to occur mainly in Pacific island societies, where large wild mammals are scarce or absent. These creatures are taken individually at some risk, no doubt adding to the prestige of the hunter/fisher.

Hunting can be difficult and dangerous. In most places, it is not the easiest way to get food and often not even the easiest way to get protein. Why, then, do hunters hunt? Why do they continue to hunt when they have domestic animals and plants, so that subsistence is no longer an issue? And, although women often do hunt, why are hunters mostly men?

Hunting is more than just killing animals to acquire food ... the symbolic aspects of hunting are at least as important as the subsistence aspects. For us, at any rate, hunting is tied to notions of the wild and to oppositions between nature and culture. Foragers may not feel these oppositions, but they, too, define hunting as more than just acquiring animal protein. The acquisition of smaller and slower animals that can be collected fairly easily is generally not counted as hunting: The element of pursuit is critical. The Cree, for example, applied their verb "to hunt" only to moose, caribou, and bear, although they killed and ate many other wild species. The San count as hunting only the killing of large game animals with the bow and arrow, a masculine undertaking, whereas women procure meat in other ways.

Recent work in primatology suggests that hunting in chimpanzees is tied not to dietary need (hunting occurs in times of plenty, not scarcity) nor to reproductive success through giving meat to females in exchange for sex. Instead, hunting, which is primarily a male activity, is related to male bonding. Meat is exchanged among males to build coalitions. Anthropoid hunting is thus political in its very origins. This explains, in part, the association of hunting with males in anthropoids, which is not the case in carnivores. Although it may seem natural to us because we are so accustomed to it in our own species, it is not obvious why hunting, rather than other activities, should promote male bonding in chimps. In animals that are now often believed to have some degree of consciousness, the symbolic statement of domination over others may be the key appeal of hunting for chimpanzee males. Moreover, this domination is achieved through cooperation.

We cannot ignore the social and symbolic aspects of hunting if we seek to explain hunting strategies. These variables enter into hunters' decisions as much as ecological factors. The very concept of hunting strategies, and indeed of optimal foraging, implies that human hunters do not simply opportunistically kill any animal they encounter, but rather make choices of what to seek and what to kill. These choices are not shaped solely by considerations of maximizing meat yield or maintaining a sustainable yield. In interpreting faunal remains, we must consider that hunters may have gained prestige by killing certain (often large) animals and that hunting may have been pursued because it bolstered notions of humanity and masculinity, even when it was not the optimal way to obtain nutrients.

Once domestic animals become the major source of meat (which may occur quite a long time after animal domestication, as herders seek to conserve their flocks by acquiring meat elsewhere), hunting can be seen as a sport. The ideology created to justify the killing of wild animals becomes a reason to continue killing them when the hunt is no longer necessary to acquire meat. Because of that ideology, game is valued more highly than the meat of domestic animals, and hunting often becomes the privilege of the elite.

The line between subsistence hunting and sport hunting is fuzzy. Because prestige and the construction of male identity are involved in most hunting, it is rarely just about subsistence. After an initial decline with the inception of herding, hunting often increases again, frequently accompanied by more elaborate ritual and symbolism.

Hunting is often ritualized in various ways, particularly in the observation of proper behavior before and during the hunt and the proper treatment of the prey. Elite hunting carries strong symbolic value and is generally quite ritualized, so that the distinction between ritual and sport hunting, especially in the premodern period, may be slight.

Sport hunting retains many of the features of subsistence hunting and is not always easily separated from it. However, the elite can appropriate the prestige inherent in hunting, especially large game hunting, for the new purposes of laying claim to territory and sovereignty."[364]

---

[364] RUSSELL 2012, 155–168.

VIII. Prescriptions and Rituals Surrounding Hunting

Hunting and fishing among hunter-gatherers gave rise to a series of prescriptions and rituals, which are regarded as essential for the success of these activities and are therefore strictly observed. The underlying notion is that animals, plants, trees, rocks and everything else in the landscape is regarded as a living person possessing an individual soul and obeying at the same time some supranatural spirit or master. Animals and topographical features of the landscape communicate to the experienced hunter promises, warnings and threats of these spiritual beings and it is the hunter's duty to know them and to show proper respect to each. In order to communicate with the appropriate supranatural powers, the hunter adapts rites derived from formulae used in corresponding situations in earlier times and refined by successive generations to meet changing needs and circumstances. It is not surprising therefore that these rituals cannot be understood properly by anyone not brought up in that culture.[365]

The tabooistic rules concern not only the hunters themselves, but most often the women of the community and regulate their behaviour before and during the hunt. Several examples are known from the Eskimos.[366] One of the most important general rules is that the hunter should avoid any kind of contact with menstruating women, who are considered as unclean and repelling the animals, and there is evidence that game animals are in fact frightened by the smell of human menses, or blood in general.[367] Women are therefore strictly segregated from the hunters and sexual abstinence is a vital requirement for hunters. It is perhaps unnecessary to repeat all the examples collected by Frazer. Instead, I quote only a short passage as *pars pro toto*:

„The Sia, a tribe of Pueblo Indians, observe chastity for four days before a hunt as well as the whole time that it lasts, even if the game be only rabbits. Among the Tsetsaut Indians of British Columbia, hunters who desire to secure good luck fast and wash their bodies with ginger-root for three or four days, and do not touch a woman for two or three months. A Shuswap Indian, who intends to go out hunting must also keep away from his wife, or he would have no luck. Among the Thompson Indians the grisly-bear hunter must abstain from sexual intercourse for some time before he went forth to hunt."[368]

---

[365] HONKO 1994, 118.
[366] HAASE 1987, 72–77.
[367] RUSSELL 2012, 161 with further references.
[368] FRAZER 1911, 197–198.

The strong persistence of some hunting rituals and taboos was already observed by Frazer: „To judge by the legislation of the Pentateuch, the ancient Semites appear to have passed through a course of moral evolution not unlike that which we can still detect in process among the Esquimaux of Baffin Land. Some of the old laws of Israel are clearly savage taboos of a familiar type thinly disguised as commands of the deity. This disguise is indeed a good deal more perfect in Palestine than in Baffin Land, but in substance it is the same. Among the Esquimaux it is the will of Sedna; among the Israelites it is the will of Jehovah."[369]

Because animals are generally believed to have souls similar to that of humans, the most important ceremonies are conducted after the actual hunt in order to propitiate them or rather their divine master/mistress in order to secure future generations of animals and success of future hunts. This is the basic principle of animal ceremonialism, observed all over the world, especially in connection with bears.[370]

In many regions, e.g. Siberia and Alaska the rites accompanying the funerals of the game animals could last several days. During this time, dances and different plays or spectacles were performed by masked hunters. One of the most important feasts was the bladder-festival, usually celebrated at full moon once a year in honour of all the animals killed, this with the object of reviving the animals for future hunts. During the days of the ceremonies, all intercourse with women is avoided. Similar funeral ceremonies were held for single (typically dangerous) game animals as well.[371] Again, a nice example has already been described in detail by Frazer:

„These fisherfolk (of Annam), we are told, worship the whale on account of the benefits they derive from it. There is hardly a village on the sea-shore which has not its small pagoda, containing the bones, more or less authentic, of a whale. When a dead whale is washed ashore, the people accord it a solemn burial. The man who first caught sight of it acts as chief mourner, performing the rites which as chief mourner and heir he would perform for a human kinsman. He puts on all the garb of woe, the straw hat, the white robe with long sleeves turned inside out, and the other paraphernalia of full mourning. As next of kin to the deceased he presides over the funeral rites. Perfumes are burned, sticks of incense kindled, leaves of gold and silver scattered, crackers let off. When the flesh has been cut off

---

[369] FRAZER 1911, 219.
[370] HALLOWELL 1926.
[371] PAULSON – HULTKRANTZ – JETTMAR 1962, 386.

and the oil extracted, the remains of the carcase are buried in the sand. Afterwards a shed is set up and offerings are made in it."[372]

Customs of Obugric peoples in Siberia (Ostjaks/Chanti, Woguls/Mansi) seem to be especially relevant in many respect: Ceremonies carried out in order to mitigate the souls of the hunted bears, were described in detail already during the 18th century and included elaborate dramatic performances.[373] Moreover, the animal souls are represented in great quantities at their cult places in the form of small wooden figurines or scratches in the tree trunks. Siberian shamans also made extensive use of wooden animal figurines.[374]

The feasts celebrated after each hunt may develop into more elaborate festivals detached from the actual hunt. The Gilyak in Siberia and the Ainu in Japan celebrate bear festivals, when the animal is brought up in captivity and is sacrificed affording „an opportunity for widely separated members of the clan to meet and share various social pleasures, the more so as the ceremonies are usually followed by games and sports of different kinds."[375] The social role of these bear festivals have already been compared to the Olympic Games.[376]

---

[372] FRAZER 1911, 223.
[373] HONKO 1994, 120–139.
[374] KARJALAINEN 1927, 5–6; HOLMBERG 1927, 83–99; 510–512; PAULSON – HULTKRANTZ – JETTMAR 1962, 93.
[375] CZAPLICKA 1904, 46.
[376] STERNBERG 1905, 260.

IX. The Cult of Artemis at Geometric Olympia

Since in historic times the main god of the sanctuary was Zeus, one is inclined to suppose that this was so from the sanctuary's very beginnings, but it is actually equally possible that there was a change in this respect. As the written sources present only late speculations on this matter, they need not be taken into consideration. The archaeological remains are more explicit in this respect: during the 7th century BC, a major reorganization of the sacred precinct took place, which was accompanied by a change in the dedicatory practices as well. Instead of the animal figurines typical for the earliest periods, arms and armour begin to be dedicated, and from the 6th century, dedicatory inscriptions attest the cult of Zeus. A huge new temple was constructed directly on the previous cult centre and votive offerings of the preceding period were dismembered and dumped into the soil. As the discussion below will show, there was a major change in the sacrificial practice as well, which does not necessarily mean for certain that the venerated god was changed, but could be reasonably explained by such a hypothesis.

However, both lines of reasoning which were put forward to account for the above facts assume that the cult of Zeus already dominated the sanctuary before this change. According to the first hypothesis, the altar was simply cleaned and old offerings were somehow deliberately dismembered and partly used as rubbish to level the terrain.[377] The reason for the great change is either unexplained or attributed to damage by lightning.[378] The other, most recent theory assumes the existence of an old altar, supposedly the centre of the cult of Zeus, being displaced during the construction of the temple (also erected for Zeus) immediately to the north of the old altar.[379]

Now, the latter hypothesis is unlikely for several reasons. First of all, a displacement of the major altar in order to make room for a new temple is not paralleled at other sites and the temple was, according to ancient tradition (Paus. 5.16.1), dedicated not to Zeus, but to Hera.[380] Moreover, the new temple was not aligned with the "new", great ash altar of Zeus located at equal distance from the

---

[377] MALLWITZ 1972, 85–87.
[378] RAMBACH 2002, 131–132.
[379] KYRIELEIS 2006.
[380] MOUSTAKA 2002 has suggested that the temple was originally built for Zeus. This theory is nowadays accepted by many scholars, but is not well-founded and misleading in my view. For a detailed discussion see PATAY-HORVÁTH 2013.

Heraion and the Pelopion (Paus. 5.13.8), but was accompanied by an own stone altar, which was erected at the same time and directly in front of the building.[381] Since there is no compelling reason to connect both altars with the cult of Zeus, the stone one in front of the Heraion was most probably dedicated to the same god as the temple itself, i.e. Hera. If the temple had been erected for Zeus and the altar had been moved as a consequence of the temple construction, one new altar would have been sufficient and one would certainly expect the "new" displaced ash altar to have been positioned directly in front of the new building.[382]

So, the main altar is likely to have remained in its original location, but questions remain to be asked pertaining to its date. That the geometric finds are conspicuously thinly represented in this area is not easily explained by the assumption that it was cleaned and the votives were swept away. And it is particularly unlikely that major cleaning of the altar became necessary at this time, but never again during following centuries. The radical rearrangement of the sanctuary suggests some more substantial change than a simple cleaning of the altar and moreover it should be acknowledged that the layer of ash does not necessarily prove the existence of a single large altar. The early ash altar is merely a hypothesis, which explains the genesis of the black stratum only if we accept that it was completely destroyed. Instead of assuming the construction and the subsequent demolition of such an altar, it is more reasonable to propose that there was none. The large area covered by ash and votives did not necessarily result from a single act of cleaning or demolishing a large altar, but could have been generated over a long period of time, when many small fireplaces were operating close to each other in this area. This scenario is not just a theoretical possibility, but is strongly supported by the evidence available at Kato Syme on Crete and on the Kynortion near Epidauros. This kind of worshipping seems to have been typical during the Bronze Age and was replaced by ceremonies at a single altar in the Iron Age.[383]

---

[381] MOUSTAKA 2013, 117–119.

[382] MOUSTAKA 2013, 119–121 assumes therefore that the stone altar was the direct successor of the hypothetical "old" altar of Zeus and was moved again afterwards to the great ash altar described by Pausanias. This sequence could eliminate the problem of two contemporary altars of Zeus standing immediately next to each other, but would at the same time mean a double displacement of the main altar and moreover a change from ash to stone and another one from stone to ash. In addition, this chronological scheme would also mean a change of the worshipped deity on the stone altar. In sum, the hypothesis seems to be rather complicated and therefore not very plausible.

[383] BERGQUIST 1988 esp. 30–34.

The sudden change in the dedicatory practices, i.e. the removal and misuse of the old votives and the genesis of the black layer can thus most probably be explained by assuming a major shift in the cult practice. It is not clear if the construction of the new temple of Hera with its stone altar and the establishment of the ash altar for Zeus were directly connected to this change, but it is certainly very likely, given the fact that both can roughly be dated to the same time, approximately the 7th century BC. The introduction of a new cult of Zeus and Hera replacing some other deity is therefore very probable. If the large building no. VII was correctly identified as a temple constructed during the early Iron Age, this would equally point to the same conclusion.[384] Although the building was unhesitatingly called the first temple of Zeus at Olympia, its orientation to the north actually shows that the deity worshipped in it was in all probability different from the later lord of the sanctuary.[385]

In sum, the archaeological evidence strongly suggests that prior to the cult of Zeus and Hera, there were other deities worshipped at the sanctuary. This idea is not new; it is even attested in some ancient sources, which have inspired modern researchers to formulate hypothetical cultic developments starting with goddesses associated with agriculture and fertility, e.g. Gaia and Demeter.[386] Such cults are located in fact in the northern part of the sanctuary, but it has been rightly pointed out that there is no archaeological evidence for their early existence.[387] By analysing the ritual prescricptions related to the sanctuary and to the games it was suggested above that it was actually the cult of a *potnia theron,* similar to and identified later with Artemis, which preceded that of Zeus.[388]

---

[384] RAMBACH 2002.

[385] ROBERTSON 2010, 71 assumed that the temple was dedicated to the worship of the Mother of the Gods, but as HITZL 1991, 10–12 clearly demonstrated, there is no clear evidence for assuming such an old cult of Meter at Olympia.

[386] Etym. Magnum s.v. *Elis* (p. 426): Πρὸ τοῦ Δία κτήσασθαι τὴν Ὀλυμπίαν παρὰ τῆς Γῆς, αὐτὴν παρειλήφεσαν Ἥλιός τε καὶ Κρόνος. Γνώρισμα δὲ τοῦ κτήματος κοινός ἐστι βωμὸς ἀμφοῖν αὐτοῖν ἐν Ὀλυμπίᾳ. Σύμβολον δὲ καὶ τόδε· τοῦ μὲν, ὁ Κρόνιος λόφος καλούμενος· τοῦ δὲ, ἡ Ἦλις μέχρι τοῦ νῦν καλουμένη ἐπώνυμος τοῦ θεοῦ. Weniger 1919 thus assumed the cult of Gaia; DREES 1962 and 1967 stressed the role of Demeter. HERRMANN 1962 considered the cults of Eilithyia, Aphrodite Urania, Ge und Hestia as the most ancient ones at the site and assumed that even Kronos was venerated from the earliest periods.

[387] KYRIELEIS 2006, 41 Anm. 141.

[388] The change of the worshipped deity may actually have involved, for a brief period the cult of Hera as well, but this cult was certainly not a very important one at Olympia:

To this, the evidence of the Homeric poems might be added, even if it is only an *argumentum e silentio*. It is a well-known fact that epic tradition does not even mention the sanctuary nor its Panhellenic festival, although there are many passages in which a reference might have been expected. Moreover, judging by the large number of geometric votive dedications, one has to conclude that the sanctuary must have been extremely popular during the Homeric age. The silence is therefore very puzzling and assuming that the cult centred on Zeus, who was so often invoked in epic and plays such an important role in the actions described, the problem becomes still more acute. On the other hand, if we accept the notion that at this time the main goddess of the sanctuary was Artemis, a simple and reasonable explanation can be suggested. Artemis is mentioned only sporadically and was clearly not particularly celebrated by epic. Her cult and sanctuaries are never mentioned at all[389] and therefore it is only natural that there is no reference to Olympia, however popular it actually was.

---

the Heraion itself does not necessarily attest the popularity of the cult, even if it was really dedicated to this goddess alone (cf. PATAY-HORVÁTH 2013) and there is nothing to prove that any votive objects e.g. the orientalizing cauldrons were dedicated to her (as assumed by SIMON 1998, 41 and GAUER 2000, 115–116).

[389] Clearly pointed out most recently by PETROVIC 2010.

X. Ethnographic Parallels for Pelops and Hippodameia

The motif of dismemberment followed by rejuvenation or resuscitation by cooking in a cauldron is not only found in Greek myths, like that of Pelops, Pelias or Dionysos, but seems to be widespread among very different peoples.[390] The tale of the „Haselshexe" has received a special emphasis,[391] although it is not a very close parallel for Pelops' boiling: the person resurrected is a female one and she dies shortly after her resurrection.

Shaman stories use the similar motif of dismemberment, cooking and resurrection, and occasionally the characteristic feature of the missing part as well. „Among the tribes of the Tungus region of Siberia, the spirits of shamanizing ancestors carry out the sparagmos. They eat the flesh of the 'slain' man raw, and only after this process can he become a shaman. Eliade quotes accounts of the (imagined) dissection of a Yakut shaman-candidate while in a state of trance and of a Samoyed candidate, the pieces of whose body were placed in a cauldron."[392] I think it would be unwise to conclude from this evidence that Pelops was originally a shaman.

The best parallels for Pelops' cauldron story can be found in the AaTh/ATU tale type no. 750B, which is about the slaughtering, eating and subsequent resurrection of an animal:

1) In the Edda, Thor and Loki arrive at a peasant family and stay there for a night. Thor slaughters his he-goats and cooks the meat in a cauldron. When serving the meal, he puts the goat hide next to the cauldron and orders everybody to preserve the bones intact and put them on the hide. The son of the peasant, Thjalfi, does not obey and splits one of the leg bones in order to get the marrow out of it. In the morning, Thor resurrects the animals from the hide and the bones and it becomes apparent that one bone is missing, because one he-goat has a limp.[393]

---

[390] THOMPSON 1958 D 1884–1885 (Rejuvenation by dismemberment / boiling), E30 (Resuscitation by arrangement of members), E 33 (Resuscitation with missing member).

[391] SCHMIDT 1963, 145–155.

[392] BUTTERWORTH 1966, 138–139 referring to the more detailed discussion by ELIADE 1968. Further references also in UHSADEL-GÜLKE 1972, 23–24.

[393] Die jüngere Edda. (Translated by G. Neckel and F. Niedner), Jena 1925, 91–92. Also quoted by SCHMIDT 1963, 127–128 with several parallels.

2) An Armenian story tells of a hunter, who was present at a marriage of the spirits of the wood. Invited to the banquet, he abstained from eating, but retained the rib of an ox which was offered to him. The bones of the animal were then re-assembled so that it might be resuscitated, but for the rib the spirits were obliged to substitute a branch of a nut tree.[394]

3) Albanian folktale: the devil spirits feasted on an ox and resuscitated it afterwards from its bones, but they were observed by a boy, who took one bone from the animal's leg. The ox therefore had a limp, until the boy reinserted the missing bone.

4) A German folktale from Allgäu: The ghosts of the night slaughter an ox and feast on it but take care that all the bones remain intact. Afterwards they put the bones together into the skin of the animal, which is thus resurrected, but somehow one leg is missing and it limps.

5) Another tale from Tirol: a hunter is invited by three witches to feast with them on a chamois, which they cook in a bronze cauldron. The witches also remind the hunter not to damage any of the bones because it would harm the animal, but he swallows one by chance. On the next day he sees a limping chamois and after three years he actually manages to catch it and realizes that it was the same animal he ate and was resurrected by the witches.[395]

In the above tales, the resurrection is shown in isolation, but there is also a nice example for the context, which clearly shows that the resurrection is not to be placed at the beginning but at the end of the life of the resurrected animal. Lapps in the 18th century explained the reason for their bear feasts by the following tale: „Three brothers had an only sister who was so hated by her brothers that she had to take refuge in the wilds. When exhausted, she finally comes across a bear's den. She enters it to have some rest; a bear comes to the same lair and, on closer acquaintance, he weds her and begets a son by her. After a while when the bear has become old and his son is grown up, the bear ... wishes to go out so as to enable the three brothers to kill him. .... When the three brothers have felled the bear and all the meat has been put in the cauldron to be boiled, the son arrives .... and says that it was his father ... and that he has therefore a right to an equal share in the bear with them. When they keep on refusing to give him this, the son

---

[394] BUTTERWORTH 1966, 141–142.
[395] UHSADEL-GÜLKE 1972, 28 with further references.

threatens to wake up his father, and then he takes a rod and saying the words, 'My father, arise! My father, arise! ', he beats the skin with it. Then the meat in the cauldron begins to boil so violently that it looks as though it wants to rise up out of the cauldron and so they are forced to give him an equal share."[396]

In sum, these parallels strongly suggest that Pelops was actually an animal and that his resurrection could well be preceeded by other episodes, like the one involving Hippodameia.

The abduction of Hippodameia seems to belong to the tale type commonly referred to as the magic flight (AaTh / ATU 313). But considering that the abductor was rather an animal, the myth of Europa and the bull comes to mind and suggests that the best and most significant ethnographic parallel could be found in the tales surrounding Sedna. There are many different versions of her myth, which is widespread among all Eskimos. The one recorded on the Baffin Island told of a young girl named Sedna, „who refused to marry any of the young men who came to woo her. In the spring, at the breaking up of the ice, a fulmar flew from over the ice and enticed Sedna to come with him by promises of a luxurious life in the land of the birds. After a long and hard journey across the sea, Sedna learned that she had been deceived. She had to live on fish and sleep in a tent covered with fish skins instead of eating meat and living in a warm hide-covered tent. Regretting her rejection of the Eskimo youths, she sang a song of woe to her father.

After a year, Sedna's father came to visit her. She begged him to take her home and told of her miserable existence. Enraged, he killed the fulmar, took Sedna in his boat and left for their home. The fulmar's companions discovered his body and flew after the fugitives. They soon saw the boat and stirred up a heavy storm, which threatened the lives of Sedna and her father. Wishing to save his own life, Sedna's father decided to offer her to the fulmars by throwing her overboard. She clung to the side of the boat, so her father took his knife and cut off the joints of her fingers one at a time. They were transformed into whales, seals and bearded seals.

Thinking Sedna had drowned, the fulmars flew away, calming the storm. Sedna was then allowed into the boat for the journey home, but she harboured a grudge against her father. When they arrived home, she called her dogs and let them gnaw off the feet and hands of her sleeping father. He woke, cursed himself, Sedna and the dogs, causing the earth to open up and swallow them all. They

---

[396] EDSMAN 1956 with several similar tales. Quotation: pp. 47–48.

now live in the land of the dead, Adlivun, where Sedna is the mistress. In other versions, Sedna was killed by her father and sank to the bottom of the sea. Her father then went home alone and, while sleeping, was swept into the sea, where he joined his daughter.

In the Dog-husband myth prevalent along the Northwest Coast, a girl took a dog for her secret lover, gave birth to puppies and was deserted by her tribe. She changed the puppies into human children who eventually provided food for the tribe which had previously rejected them. In the Eskimo version, the girl refused to marry and was given a dog as her husband. She gave birth to several offspring before or after her father moved her to an island. Her husband obtained their food from her father, who finally killed him. ... The Sedna myth and the Dog-husband myth were sometimes joined, placing the marriage to the dog before the marriage to the bird. ... The Sedna myth appears to have undergone a series of changes. Erik Holtved traced the development of the Sedna myth, concluding that it originally consisted of two myths, the Storm Bird and the Kayak-Ferry. The Storm Bird is similar to the Sedna myth except that all the occupants of the boat are drowned in the storm caused by the bird, and no sea animals are created. In the Kayak-Ferry myths, an orphan girl or old widow tried to board boats carrying members of the group to another hunting ground. She was thrown overboard and her fingers chopped off. The parts of the fingers became various sea animals, and the girl or old woman was identified as Sedna. Holtved maintained that the two myths were combined to form the present Sedna myth, and the combination with the Dog-Husband myth is a further development."[397]

Notwithstanding the differences in the mythical tales concerning Sedna, she was the central figure of Eskimo rituals in general and a series of taboos was attached to her cult. As the sea animals were created from her fingers, she was the mistress of the these animals and lived on the bottom of the sea in a house, where the souls of the dead animals returned. They informed her whether the eskimos respected the taboos; if they did not, she withheld the animals and hunting became unsuccessful. In order to appease her, the shaman has to travel to her, comb and clean her hair, or even fight with her, so that she might release the souls of the animals again.[398]

---

[397] FISHER 1975, 28–32.
[398] Cf. e.g. FRAZER 1911, 210–211.

Abbreviations

AA	Archäologischer Anzeiger
AEphem	Archaiologiké Ephémeris
AJA	American Journal of Archaeology
AM	Mitteilungen des Deutschen Archäologischen Instituts, Athenische Abteilung
Arch. Hom	Archaeologia Homerica
BCH	Bulletin de Correspondance Hellénique
DNP	Der Neue Pauly
EM	Enzyclopädie des Märchens
JdI	Jahrbuch des Deutschen Archäologischen Instituts
GRBS	Greek, Roman and Byzantine Studies
OlForsch	Olympische Forschungen
LIMC	Lexicon Iconographicum Mythologiae Classicae
RE	Pauly-Wissowa Realenzyclopädie der klassischen Altertumswissenschaft
ThesCRA	Thesaurus Cultus et Rituum Antiquorum

Bibliography

Ameling, W. 2000. s.v. Pelops [2], in: *DNP* Vol. 9, p. 510.

Andrews, Tamsey K. 1994. *Bronzecasting at Geometric period Olympia and Early Greek Metal Sources*, PhD Dissertation Brandeis University.

Aruz, J. et al. (eds) 2008. *Beyond Babylon: Art, Trade, and Diplomacy in the Second Millennium B.C., Exhibition Catalogue of the Metropolitan Museum of Art, New York*, New Haven–London.

Athanassopoulou, S. et al. 2003. *Bull in the Mediterranean World. Myths and Cults*, Exhibition Catalogue Athens – Barcelona.

Auffarth, Chr. 1998. Fest, Festkultur, in: *DNP* 4, 483–493.

Baitinger, H. 2011. *Waffenweihungen in griechischen Heiligtümern,* Mainz.

Baitinger, H. – Völling, Th. 2007. *Werkzeug und Gerät aus Olympia* (OlForsch 32) Berlin.

Barringer, J. 2001. *The Hunt in Ancient Greece*, Baltimore.

Bauer, J. 1993. Jägerzeitliche Vorstellungen, in: EM Vol. 7, 427–432.

Baumbach, J. D. 2004. *The significance of votive offerings in selected Hera sanctuaries in the Peloponnese, Ionia and Western Greece* (BAR 1249). Oxford.

Beekes, R. S. P. 2010. *Etymological dictionary of Greek I–II*, Leiden.

Benecke, N. 2006a. Die Tierreste, in: H. Kyrieleis (ed.), *Anfänge und Frühzeit des Heiligtums von Olympia* (OlForsch 31) Berlin, 247–248.

Benecke, N. 2006b. Animal Sacrifice at Late Archaic Artemision of Olympia. The Archaeological evidence, in: U. Tecchiati – B. Sala (eds), *Archaeozoological Studies in Honour of Alfredo Riedel*, Bolzano, 153–160.

Benkő, L. 1966. Az anonymusi hagyomány — és a Csepel név eredete, *Magyar Nyelv* 62, 134–146; 292–305.

Benton, S. 1935. The evolution of the tripod-lebes, *Annual of the British School at Athens* 35, 74–130.

Bergquist, B. 1988. The archaeology of sacrifice. Minoan-Mycenaean versus Greek, in: R. Hägg – N. Marinatos – G. C. Nordquist (eds), *Early Greek Cult Practice*, Stockholm, 21–34.

Bevan, E. 1986. *Representations of Animals in Sanctuaries of Artemis and other Olympian Deities* (BAR Int. 315), Oxford

Bile, M. 1992. Les termes relatifs à l'initiation dans les inscriptions crétoises (vii–i siecles av. J-C.), in: A. Moreau (ed), *L initiation. Les rites d'adolescence et mystères*, Montpellier, 11–18.

Boardman, J. 2002. *The Archaeology of Nostalgia*, London.

Bol, P. C. 2002. Protogeometrische – Spätgeometrische Plastik, in: P.C. Bol (ed.), *Die Geschichte der antiken Bildhauerkunst I. Frühgriechische Plastik*, Mainz, 3–21.

Borgeaud, Ph. 1979. *Recherches sur le dieu Pan*, Genève.

Bökönyi, S. 1974. *History of domesticated mammals in Central and Eastern Europe*, Budapest.

Bötticher, C. 1856. *Der Baumkultus der Hellenen*, Berlin.

Brednich, R.W. 1977. Anthropomorphisierung, in: EM Vol. 1, 591–596.

Brelich, A. 1969. *Paides e parthenoi*, Roma.

Brown, C. 1982, Dionysus and the Women of Elis: "PMG" 871, *GRBS* 23, 305–314.

Brulé, P. 1992. Fêtes grecques: périodicité et initiations. Hyakinthies et Panathénées. in: A. Moreau (ed.), *L'initiation. Les rites d'adolescence et les mystères*, Montpellier, 19–38.

Buchholz, H-G. et al. 1973. *Jagd und Fischfang* (Arch. Hom II J), Göttingen.

Burkert, W. 1972. *Homo necans*, Berlin.

Burkert, W. 1979. *Structure and History in Greek Mythology and Ritual*, Berkeley.

Burkert, W. 1988. Heros, Tod und Sport : Ritual und Mythos der Olympischen Spiele in der Antike, in G. Gebauer (ed.), *Körper- und Einbildungskraft. Inszenierungen des Helden im Sport*. Berlin, 31–42 (= F. Graf (ed.), W. Burkert, *Kleine Schriften V. Mythica, Ritualia, Religiosa 2*, Göttingen 2011, 218–230).

Burkert, W. 1992. *The Orientalizing Revolution*, Cambridge (MA).

Burkert, W. 2011. *Griechische Religion der archaischen und klassischen Epoche*, Stuttgart.

Butterworth, E. A. S. 1966. *Some Traces of the Pre-Olympian World in Greek Literature and Myth*, Berlin.

Canosa, J. A. F. 1994. Pélope: la maduración de un país, *Polis* 6, 53–74.

Chaniotis, A. 2011. Greek festivals and contests: definition and general characteristics, in: *ThesCRA* VII, 4–42.

Chantraine, P. 1956. *Études sur le vocabulaire grec*. Paris.

Chantraine, P. 1999. *Dictionnaire étymologique de la langue grecque*, Paris.

Cherry, J. F. 1988. Pastoralism and the Role of Animals in the Pre- and Protohistoric Economies of the Aegean, in: C. R. Whittaker (ed.), *Pastoral Economies in Classical Antiquity* (Cambridge Philological Society, Suppl. Vol. No. 14), 177–195.

Christesen, P. 2007. *Olympic Victor Lists and Ancient Greek History*, Cambridge.

Clark, M. 2013. *Exploring Greek Myth*, Oxford –Malden.

Clutton-Brock, J. 1999. *A Natural History of Domesticated Mammals*, Cambridge.

Coldstream, N. 2003. *Geometric Greece 900–700 B.C.*, London–New York.

Comstock, M. – C. Vermeule 1971. *Greek, Etruscan and Roman Bronzes in the Museum of Fine Arts*, Boston.

Cook, A. B. 1904. The European Sky-God, *Folk-Lore* 15, 264–315; 369–426.

Cook, E. F. 1995. *The Odyssey in Athens*. Ithaca.

Cornford, F. M. 1927. The Origin of the Olympic Games, in: J. E. Harrison, *Themis. A Study of the Social Origins of Greek Religion*, Cambridge, 212–259.

Cuche, V. 2014. Le coureur et le guerrier. Anthropologie de la course à pied et de ses vertus militaires, *Kernos* 27, 9–50.

Culin, S. 1907. *24th Annual report of the Bureau of American Ethnology: Games of the North American Indians.* Washington DC.

Czaplicka, M. A. 1904. *Aboriginal Siberia*, Oxford.

Dalgat, U. B. 1979. Brautraub in: EM Vol. 2, 753–762.

de Polignac, F. 1996. Offrandes, mémoire et compétition ritualisée dans les sanctuaires grecs à l'époque géometrique, in: P. Hellström – B. Alroth (eds), *Religion and Power in the Ancient Greek World*, Uppsala 59–66.

de Ridder, A. 1896. *Catalogue des bronzes trouvés sur l'Acropole d'Athènes*, Paris.

Decker, W. 1995. *Sport in der griechischen Antike*, München.

Detienne, M. 1977. *Dionysos mis à mort*, Paris.

Devereux, G. 1965. The abduction of Hippodameia as „aition" of a Greek animal husbandry rite, Studi e Materiali di Storia delle Religioni 36, 3–25 (= idem, *Femme et mythe*, Paris, 1982, 216–234 / *Frau und Mythos*, München, 1986, 241–267).

Dietrich, B. C. 1974. *The Origins of Greek Religion*, Berlin.

di Lernia, S. – M. Gallinaro 2010. The date and context of Neolithic rock art in the Sahara: engravings and ceremonial monuments from Messak Settafet (south-west Libya), *Antiquity* 84, 954–975.

Dillon, M. 2001. Girls and Women in classical Greek Religion, London–New York

Dowden, K. 2011. Initiation: The Key to Myth?, in: K. Dowden – N. Livingstone (eds), *A Companion to Greek Mythology*, Malden, 487–505.

Drees, L. 1962. *Der Ursprung der Olympischen Spiele*, Stuttgart.

Drees, L. 1967. *Olympia. Götter, Künstler und Athleten*, Stuttgart.

Dugas, Ch. 1921. Le sanctuaire d'Aléa Athéna à Tégée avant le IVe siècle, *BCH* 45, 335–435.

Duncan, P. 1992. *Horses and grasses; the nutritional ecology of equids and their impact on the Camargue*, New York.

Eder, B. 2006. The World of Telemachus: Western Greece 1200–700 BC, in S. Deger-Jalkotzy and I. S. Lemos (eds), *Ancient Greece. From the Mycenean Palaces to the Age of Homer*, Edinburgh, 549–580.

Edsman, C. M. 1956. The Story of the Bear wife in Nordic tradition, *Ethnos* 21, 36–56.

Ekroth, G. 2012. Pelops Joins the Party. Transformations of a Hero Cult within the Festival at Olympia, in: J. R. Brandt – J. W. Iddeng (eds), *Greek and Roman Festivals. Content, Meaning and Practice*, Oxford, 95–137.

Eliade, M. 1968. *Le Chamanisme*, Paris.

Farnell, L. R. 1896(-1909). *The Cults of the Greek States*, Oxford.

Fehrle, B. 1910. *Die kultische Keuschheit im Altertum*, Gießen.

Fick, A. – Bechtel, F. 1894. *Die griechischen Personennamen nach ihrer Bildung erklärt und systematisch geordnet*, Göttingen.

Fisher, J. F. 1975. An Analysis of the Central Eskimo Sedna Myth, *Temenos* 11, 27–42.

Fontenrose, J. 1981. *Orion: The Myth of the Hunter and the Huntress*, Berkeley.

Forstenpointer, G. 2003. Promethean legacy: investigations into the ritual procedure of 'Olympian' sacrifice, in: E. Kotjabopoulou (ed.), *Zooarchaeology in Greece. Recent advances* (British School at Athens studies No. 9) London, 203–213.

Frazer, J. G. 1911. Taboo. *The Perils of the Soul (=The Golden bough Part II)*, London.

Frenzel, E. 1987. Freier, Freierproben, in: EM Vol. 5, 227–236.

Frisk, H. 1973. *Griechisches etymologisches Wörterbuch*, Heidelberg.

Furtwängler, A. 1890. *Die Bronzen und die übrigen kleineren Funde von Olympia*, Berlin.

Gangloff, A. 2012. La dévoration de Pélops: de l'infanticide au modèle politique et social, in: S. Dubel – A. Montandon (eds), *Mythes sacrificiels et ragoûts d'enfants*, Clermont-Ferrand, 87–99.

Gardiner, E. N. 1925. *Olympia: Its History and Remains*, Oxford.

Gauer, W. 1991. *Die Bronzegefässe von Olympia: mit Ausnahme der geometrischen Dreifüsse und der Kessel des orientalisierenden Stils* (OlForsch 20), Berlin.

Gauer, W. 2000, Olympia, der Orient und Etrurien, in F. Prayon – W. Röllig (eds), *Der Orient und Etrurien. Zum Phänomen des Orientalisierens im westlichen Mittelmeerraum, 10. – 6. Jh. v.Chr. Akten des Kolloquiums,* Pisa, 113–128.

Gernet, L. 1981. Value in Greek myth, in: R. Gordon (ed.), *Myth, Religion and Society: Structuralist Essays by M. Detienne, L. Gernet, J.-P. Vernant and P. Vidal-Naquet*, Cambridge, 111–146. (originally published as „La notion mythique de la valeur en Grèce", *Journal de psychologie* 41, 1948, 415–462.)

Gobrecht, B. 1996. Köpfe auf Pfählen, in: EM Vol. 8, 264–268.

Golden, M. 1998. *Sport and Society in Ancient Greece*, Cambridge.

Graf, F. 2003. Initiation: a concept with a troubled history, in: D. B. Dodd – Chr. Faraone (eds), *Initiation in ancient Greek rituals and narratives. New critical perspectives*, London, 3–24.

Grottanelli, C. 1984. Ospitare gli dei: sacrificio e diluvio, *Studi Storici* 25, 847–857.

Gruppe, O. 1906. *Griechische Mythologie und Religionsgeschichte*, München.

Guggisberg, M. A. 1996. *Frühgriechische Tierkeramik: zur Entwicklung und Bedeutung der Tiergefäße und der hohlen Tierfiguren in der späten Bronze- und frühen Eisenzeit (ca. 1600 – 700 v. Chr.)*, Mainz.

Guggisberg, M. A. 2005. Der Krieger als Jäger: Zur Bedeutung der Jagd in den 'Dark Ages', in A. Alexandridis et al. (eds), *Mensch und Tier in der Antike*, Wiesbaden 2008, 329–352.

Guidorizzi, G. (ed.) 2000. *Igino, Miti*, Milano.

Haase, E. 1987. *Der Schmanismus der Eskimos*, Aachen.

Hägg, R. 1998. Osteology and Greek sacrificial practice, in: R. Hägg (ed.), *Ancient Greek cult practice from the Archaeological Evidence*, Stockholm 49–56.

Hallowell, A. I. 1926. Bear Ceremonialism in the Northern Hemisphere, *American Anthropologist* 28, 1–175.

Halm-Tisserant, M. 1993. *Cannibalism et immortalité. L'enfant dans le chaudron en Grèce ancienne*. Paris.

Hamilakis, Y. 2003. The sacred geography of hunting: wild animals, social power and gender in early farming societies, in: E. Kotjabopoulou (ed.), *Zooarchaeology in Greece. Recent advances* (British School at Athens studies No. 9) London, 239–247.

Hannah, R. 2005. *Greek and Roman Calendars*, London.

Harrison, J. E. 1927. *Themis. A Study of the Social Origins of Greek Religion*, Cambridge.

Heath, J. 2011. Animals, in: M. Finkelberg (ed.), *The Homer Encyclopedia*, Malden, 56–57.

Heiden, J. 2012. Artemis-Altäre, in W-D. Heilmeyer et al. (eds), *Mythos Olympia. Ausstellungskatalog Martin-Gropius-Bau*, Berlin, 145–147.

Heilmeyer, W-D. 1972. *Frühe Olympische Tonfiguren* (OlForsch 7) Berlin.

Heilmeyer, W-D. 1979. *Frühe Olympische Bronzefiguren. Die Tiervotive* (OlForsch 12). Berlin.

Heilmeyer, W-D. 1994. Frühe olympische Bronzefiguren. Die Wagenvotive, in: E. Kunze, E. Kunze-Götte, A. Mallwitz (eds), *IX. Bericht über die Ausgrabungen in Olympia. Herbst 1962 bis Frühjahr 1966*, Berlin, 172–208.

Herrmann, H-V. 1962. Zur ältesten Geschichte Olympias, *AM* 77, 3–34.

Herrmann, H-V. 1964. Werkstätten geometrischer Bronzeplastik, *JdI* 79, 17–71.

Herrmann, H-V. 1966. *Die Kessel der orientalisierenden Zeit I* (OlForsch 6), Berlin.

Herrmann, H-V. 1972. *Olympia. Heiligtum und Wettkampfstätte*, München.

Herrmann, H-V. 1979. *Die Kessel der orientalisierenden Zeit II* (OlForsch 11), Berlin.

Herrmann, H-V. 1980. Pelops in Olympia, in: *Stele. Tomos eis mnemen N. Kontoleontos*, Athens, 59–74.

Herrmann, H-V. 1988. Die Siegerstatuen von Olympia, *Nikephoros* 1, 119–183.

Herrmann, H-V. 1991. review of Morgan 1990, *Nikephoros* 4, 260–265.

Hill, D.K. 1955. Six Early Greek Animals, *AJA* 59, 39–44.

Himmelmann, N. 2002. Frühe Weihgeschenke, in: H. Kyrieleis (ed.), *Olympia 1875 – 2000. 125 Jahre deutsche Ausgrabungen*, Mainz 91–107.

Hitzl, K. 1991. *Die kaiserzeitliche Statuenausstattung des Metroon* (OlForsch XIX) Berlin.

Hodkinson, S. 1988. Animal husbandry in the Greek polis, in C. R. Whittaker (ed.), *Pastoral Economies in Classical Antiquity* (Cambridge Philological Society, Suppl. Vol. No. 14), 35–74.

Holmberg, U. 1927. *Finno-Ugric, Siberian Mythology*, Boston.

Honko, L. 1994. Hunting, in L. Honko et. al., *The Great Bear: A Thematic Anthology of Oral Poetry in the Finno-Ugrian Languages*, Oxford, 117–139.

Howe, T. 2008. *Pastoral politics. Animals, agriculture and society in ancient Greece*. Claremont.

Hönle, A. 1968. *Olympia in der Politik der griechischen Staatenwelt von 776 bis zum Ende des 5. Jahrhunderts.* Tübingen.

Hubbard, Th. K. 1987. The „cooking" of Pelops: Pindar and the process of mythological revisionism, *Helios* 14, 3–21.

Hughes, Donald J. 2014. *Environmental Problems of the Greeks and Romans. Ecology in the Ancient Mediterranean*, Baltimore.

Icard N. / P. Linant de Bellefonds 2011. La chasse dans le monde grec et romain, in: *ThesCRA Vol. VI,* s.v. „2.c. Chasse", Los Angeles 361–370.

Instone, S. 2007. Origins of the Olympics, in: S. Hornblower – C. Morgan (eds), *Pindar's Poetry, Patrons, and Festivals*, Oxford, 71–82.

Isler-Kerényi, C. 2007. *Dionysos in Archaic Greece*, Leiden–Boston.

Ivanov, S. W. 1959. Religiöse Vorwürfe in der Kunst der Völker Nordasiens vor der Revolution, in: *Opuscula Ethnologica Memoriae Ludovici Bíró Sacra*, Budapest, 113–136.

Janietz, B. 1989. *Untersuchungen an geometrischen Bronzen*, Diss. Freiburg (http://www.freidok.uni-freiburg.de/volltexte/199/pdf/JanietzDiss.pdf).

Jeanmaire, H. 1939. *Couroi et Courètes*, Lille.

Jost, M. 1985. *Sanctuaires et cultes d'Arcadie*. Paris.

Kahil, L. 1984. Artemis, in: *LIMC* Vol. 2, Zürich–München 618–753.

Karagiorgia, Th. G. 1972. Ανασκαφη περιοξης αρχαιου Δωριου, *AEphem* 27 Chron. 12–20.

Karjalainen, K. F. 1927. *Die Religion der Jugravölker III*, Helsinki.

Karouzos, Chr. 2000. *Περικαλλες αγαλμα εξεποιησ' ουκ αδαης,* Athena.

Kearns, E. 2011, Religion, in: M. Finkelberg (ed.), *The Homer Encyclopedia*, Malden, 735–738.

Keller, O. 1887. *Tiere des klassischen Altertums*, Innsbruck (Nachdruck: Hildesheim, 2001).

Keller, O. 1909. *Antike Tierwelt I–II*, Leipzig.

Kett, P. 1966. *Prosopographie der historischen griechischen Manteis bis auf die Zeit Alexanders des Grossen*, Diss. Nürnberg.

Kiderlen, M. 2010. Zur Chronologie griechischer Bronzedreifüsse des geometrischen Typus und den Möglichkeiten einer politisch-historischen Interpretation der Fundverteilung, *AA* 91–104.

Kirk, G. S. 1974. *The Nature of Greek Myths*, Harmondsworth.

Kitahara, M. 1982. Menstrual Taboos and the mportance of hunting, *American Anthropologist* 84, 901–903.

Konecny, A. et al. 2013. *Plataiai. Archäologie und Geschichte einer boiotischen Polis*. Wien.

Kossaifi, Chr. 2012. Aux origines mythiques de l'Arcadie. La symbolique du sacrifice d'Arcas par Lycaon, in: S. Dubel – A. Montandon (eds), *Mythes sacrificiels et ragoûts d'enfants*, Clermont-Ferrand, 101–123.

Köhler-Zülch, I. 2012. Wiederbelebung in: EM Vol. 14, 737–746.

Krappe, A. H. 1941. Picus who is also Zeus, *Mnemosyne* 9, 241–257.

Krappe, A. H. 1942. Guiding Animals, *The Journal of American Folklore* 55, 228–246.

Kretschmer, P. 1938. Literaturbericht für das Jahr 1935. Griechisch, *Glotta* 27, 1–40.

Kretschmer, P. 1940. Die vorgriechischen Sprach- und Volksschichten, *Glotta* 28, 231–278.

Kronfeld-Schor, N. et. al. 2013. Chronobiology by moonlight, *Proceedings of the Royal Society* B 280: 20123088.

Krummen, E. 1990. *Pyrsos hymnon*, Berlin.

Kyle, D. G. 2007. *Sport and Spectacle in the Ancient World*, Malden.

Kyrieleis, H. 2006. *Anfänge und Frühzeit des Heiligtums von Olympia* (OlForsch 31), Berlin.

Kyrieleis, H. 2011, *Olympia. Archäologie eines Heiligtums*. Mainz.

Kyrieleis, H. 2013. Archaische Dreifüsse in Olympia, in: H. Kyrieleis (Hrsg.), *XIII. Bericht über die Ausgrabungen in Olympia*, Tübingen/Berlin, 182–227.

Lane Fox, R. 1996. Ancient hunting: from Homer to Polybios, in: G. Shipley and J. Salmon (eds), *Human Landscapes in Classical Antiquity*, London – New York, 119–153.

Langdon, S. 1982. Review of Schmaltz 1980, *AJA* 86, 596–597.

Langdon, S. 1987a. Gift Exchange in the Geometric Sanctuaries, in: T. Linders – G. Nordquist (eds), *Gifts to the Gods*, Uppsala, 107–113.

Langdon, S. 1987b. In the Pasture of the Gods, *Muse* 21, 55–64.

Langdon, S. (ed.) 1993. *From Pasture to Polis: Art in the Age of Homer*, Columbia.

Langdon, S. 2008. *Art and identity in dark age Greece, 1100 – 700 B.C.E.*, Cambridge.

Langdon, S. 2010. Where the Wild Things Were: The Greek Master of Animals in Ecological Perspective, in: D. B. Counts – B. Arnold (eds), *The Master of Animals in World Iconography*, Budapest 119–133.

Larson, J. 1995. *Greek Heroine Cults*, Madison.

Larson, J. 2007. *Ancient Greek Cults. A Guide*, New York.

Lebessi, A. 1985 *Το ιερό του Ερμή και της Αφροδίτης στη Σύμη Βιάννου, 1, 1. Χάλκινα κρητικά τορεύματα.* (Βιβλιοθήκη της εν Αθήναις Αρχαιολογικής Εταιρείας, 102) Athen.

Lee, H. M. 1988. The „First" Olympic Games of 776 BC, in: W. J. Raschke (ed.), *The Archaeology of the Olympics*, Madison, 110–118.

Lehmann-Hartleben, K. 1939. Note on the Potnia Taurōn, *AJA* 43, 669–671.

Lengerken, H. von 1955. *Ur, Hausrind und Mensch*, Berlin.

Leroi-Gourhan, A. 1964. *Les religions de la préhistoire*, PUF.

Leroi-Gourhan, A. 1983. *Lés chasseurs de la préhistoire*. Paris.

Leroi-Gourhan, A. 1992. *L'art pariétal. Language de la préhistoire*. Grenoble

Lesky, A. 1931. Melikertes, *RE* XV,1, 514–520.

Lévêque, P. 1982. Approche ethno-historique des concours grecs, *Klio* 64, 5–20.

Lorenz, G. 2000. *Tiere im Leben der alten Kulturen*, Wien.

Maass, M. 1978. *Die geometrischen Dreifüsse von Olympia* (OlForsch 10), Berlin.

Maass, M. 1981. Die geometrischen Dreifüsse von Olympia, *Antike Kunst* 24, 1981, 6–20.

Maass, M. 1992. Frühe Weihgaben in Delphi und Olympia als Zeugnisse für die Geschichte der Heiligtümer, in: J- F. Bommelaer (ed.), *Delphes. Centenaire de la „Grande Fouille" réalisée par l'École Française d'Athènes (1892–1903),* Leiden 85–93.

Maass, M. 1993. *Das antike Delphi*, Darmstadt.

Macurdy, G. H. 1923. The Horse-taming Trojans, *Classical Quarterly* 17, 50–52.

Mallwitz, A. 1988. Cult and Competition Locations at Olympia, in: W. J. Raschke (ed.), *The Archaeology of the Olympics*, Madison 79–109.

Mallwitz, A. (bearb. von K. Herrmann) 1999. Ergebnisse und Folgerungen, in: *XI. Bericht über die Ausgrabungen in Olympia*, Berlin.

Mannhardt, W. 1905. *Wald- und Feldkulte. I. Der Baumkultus der Germanen und ihrer Nachbarstämme*, Berlin (=Nachdruck: Darmstadt, 1963)

March, K. S. 1980. Deer, Bears, and Blood: A Note on Nonhuman Animal Response to Menstrual Odor, *American Anthropologist* 82, 125–127.

Marinatos, N. 2000. *The Goddess and the Warrior, the naked goddess and Mistress of Animals in early Greek religion*. London.

Marinatos, N. 2003. Striding across boundaries: Hermes and Aphrodite as gods of initiation, in: D. B. Dodd – Chr. Faraone (eds), *Initiation in ancient Greek rituals and narratives. New critical perspectives*, London, 130–151.

Mayor, A. 2000. *The first fossil hunters. Paleontology in Greek and Roman Times,* Princeton

McInerney, J. 2010. *The Cattle of the Sun. Cows and Culture in the World of the Ancient Greeks*, Princeton.

McLennan, J. F. 1865. *Primitive marriage. An inquiry into the origin of the form of capture in marriage ceremonies*, Edinburgh.

Mellaart, J. 1967. *Çatal Hüyük. A neolithic Town in Anatolia*, London.

Meuli, K. 1941. Der Ursprung der Olympischen Spiele, *Die Antike* 17, 189–208.

Meuli, K. 1946. Griechische Opferbräuche, in: *Phyllobolia für Peter von der Mühll*, Basel 185–288 (= Gesammelte Werke, Hrsg. von Th. Gelzer, Bd. II, Basel 1975, 907–1021.)

Meuli, K. 1968. *Der griechische Agon. Kampf und Kampfspiel im Totenbrauch, Totentanz, Totenklage und Todenlob,* Köln (manuscript 1926).

Miller, S. G. 1975. The date of Olympic Festivals, *AM* 90, 215–231.

Miller, S. G. (ed.) 1989. *Nemea. A Guide to the Site and Museum.* Berkeley.

Minon, S. 2007. *Inscriptions Éléens dialectales*. Genève.

Montepaone C. 1993. L'alsos / lucus, forma idealtipica artemidea: il caso di Ippolito, in: O. de Cazanove (ed.), *Les bois sacrés*, Naples 69–75.

Moretti, L. 1957. Olimpionikai. I vincitori negli antichi agoni olimpici, *MemLinc* Ser VIII, Vol. VIII Fasc. 2.

Morgan, C. 1990. *Athletes and Oracles*, Cambridge.

Morgan, C. 1993. The origins of pan-Hellenism, in: N. Marinatos – R. Hägg (eds), *Greek sanctuaries. New approaches*, London, 14–33.

Morgan, C. 2003. *Early Greek states beyond the polis*. London–New York.

Mouratides, J. 1984. Heracles at Olympia and the Exclusion of Women from the Ancient Olympic Games, *Journal of Sport history* 11, 41–55.

Moustaka, A. 2002. Zeus und Hera im Heiligtum von Olympia und die Kulttopographie von Elis und Triphylien, in: H. Kyrieleis (ed.), *Olympia 1875 – 2000. 125 Jahre deutsche Ausgrabungen*, Mainz, 301–315.

Moustaka, A. (with K. Herrmann) 2013. Untersuchungen am Heraion-Altar, in: H. Kyrieleis (ed.), *XIII. Bericht über die Ausgrabungen in Olympia*, Tübingen/Berlin, 100–128.

Murray, S. C. 2014. The Role of Religion in Greek Sport, in: P. Christesen – D.G. Kyle (eds), *A Companion to Sport and Spectacle in Greek and Roman Antiquity*, Malden, 309–319

Nafissi, M. 2003. Elei e Pisati. Geografia, storia e istituzioni politiche della regione di Olimpia, *Geographia Antiqua* 12, 23–55.

Nagy, G. 1986. Pindar's Olympian I and the aetiology of the Olympic Games, *Transactions of the American Philological Society* 116, 71–88.

Nilsson, M. P. 1906. *Griechische Feste von religiöser Bedeutung mit Ausschluss der attischen*, Leipzig.

Nilsson, M. P. 1962. *Die Entstehung und religiöse Bedeutung des griechischen Kalenders*, Lund.

Niniou-Kindeli, V. 2003. The Bull and the Sanctuary of Poseidon at Chania, Crete, in: Athanassopoulou, S. et al. 2003, 132–137.

Nobis, G. 1996. Der Auerochse oder Ur (Bos primigenius) auf Kreta, in D. S. Reese (ed.), *Pleistocene and Holocene Fauna of Crete and its Forst Settlers* (Monographs in World Archaeology No. 28) 263–272, Madison.

Pache, C. O. 2004. *Baby and Child heroes in Ancient Greece*, Chicago.

Papathanasopoulos, G. A. 1969. Αρηαιοτητες και μνημεια Ηλειας, *Archaiologikon Deltion* 24 Chron. 146–154.

Papavasileiou, G. A. 1912. Ανασκαφαι και ερευναι εν Ευβοια, *Praktika tes en Athenais Archailogikes Hetaireias* 1912, 119–140.

Parker, R. 2007. *Polytheism and Society at Athens*, Oxford.

Patay-Horváth, A. 2013. Hera in Olympia: Tempel, Kult und Münzprägung, *Thetis* 20, 81–99.

Paulson, I. 1961. *Schutzgeister und Gottheiten des Wildes (der Jagdtiere und Fische) in Nordeurasien*. Stockholm.

Paulson, I. – Hultkrantz, A.– Jettmar, K. 1962. *Die Religionen Nordeurasiens und der amerikanischen Arktis*, Stuttgart.

Persson, P. O. 1993. Ure in Chania auf Kreta, *Tier und Museum* 3(4): 121–123. (non vidi)

Petermandl, W. 2013. Orsippos und die Einführung der athletischen Nacktheit oder: die Geschichte einer Geschichte, in: Breitwieser, R. – Frass, M. – Nightingale, G. (eds), *Calamus. Festschrift für Herbert Graßl zum 65. Geburtstag*, Wiesbaden, 349–360.

Petrovic, I. 2010. Transforming Artemis. From the Goddess of the Outdoors to City Goddess, in: Bremmer, J. N. – Erskine, A. (ed.), *The gods of ancient Greece. Identities and transformations*. Edinburgh, 209–227.

Petterson, M. 1992. *Cults of Apollo at Sparta: the Hyakinthia, the Gymnopaidiai and the Karneia*, Stockholm.

Pilali-Papasteriou, A. 1985. *Die bronzenen Tierfiguren aus Kreta* (PBF I,3), München.

Pleket, H. W. 1974. Zur Soziologie des antiken Sports, *MededRom* 36, 57–87 (= *Nikephoros* 14, 2001, 157–212).

Pötscher, W. 1990. *Aspekte und Probleme der minoischen Religion*, Hildesheim.

Prent, M. 2005, *Cretan Sanctuaries and Cults*, Leiden/Boston.

Propp, V. 1972. *Morphologie des Märchens*, München.

Propp, V. 1987. *Die historischen Wurzeln des Zaubermärchens*, München.

Puchner, W. 2002. Pelops, in: EM Vol. 10, 704–707.

Rambach, J. 2002. Dörpfelds Bau VII in der Altis von Olympia: Ein früheisenzeitliches Apsidenhaus und 'Haus des Oinomaos', *AA* 2002, 119–134.

Renaud, J.-M. 2004. *Le mythe d'Orion*, Liège.

Rice, M. 1998. *The Power of the Bull*, London–New York.

Richer, N. 1998. *Les éphores*, Paris.

Richer, N. 2011. *La religion des Spartiates*, Paris.

Richter, W. 1968. *Die Landwirtschaft im homerischen Zeitalter* (Arch. Hom. II H) Göttingen.

Robertson, N. 2010, *Religion and Reconciliation in Greek Cities: The Sacred Laws of Selinus and Cyrene*. Oxford/New York.

Robson, J. E. 2002. Bestiality and bestial rape in Greek myth, in: S. Deacy – K. F. Pierce (eds), *Rape in Antiquity*, London, 65–96.

Roller, L. E. 1981. Funeral games for historical persons, *Stadion* 7, 1–18.

Rolley, C. 1969. *Les statuettes de bronze* (Fouilles de Delphes 5.2), Paris.

Rolley C. et al. 1983. Bronzes grecs et orientaux, influences et apprentissage, *BCH* 107, 111–132.

Rolley, C. 1992. Argos, Corinthe, Athènes, in: M. Piérart (ed.), *Polydipsion Argos* (BCH Suppl. 22), Paris 37–49.

Rolley, C. 1994. *La sculpture grecque I*, Paris.

Röhrich, L. 1993. Jagd, Jagen, Jäger, in: EM Vol. 7, 394–411.

Röhrich, L. 2002. *„und weil sie nicht gestorben sind ..." Anthropologie, Kulturgeschichte und Deutung von Märchen*, Köln–Weimar–Wien.

Russell, N. 2012 *Social Zooarchaeology. Humans and Animals in Prehistory*, Cambridge.

Russell, N. and Martin, L. 2005. The Çatalhöyük mammal remains. In *Inhabiting Çatalhöyük: Reports from the 1995–1999 Seasons.* ed. by I. Hodder, 33–98.

Sallares, R. 1991. *The Ecology of the Ancient Greek World*, Ithaca.

Sansone, D. 1988. *Greek Athletics and The Genesis of Sport*, Berkeley.

Scanlon, Th. F. 2002. *Eros and Greek Athletics*, Oxford.

Schachter, A. 1994. *Cults of Boiotia* (Bulletin of the Institute of Classical Studies, supplement no. 38), London.

Schmaltz, B. 1980. *Metallfiguren aus dem Kabirenheiligtum bei Theben, Die Statuetten aus Bronze und Blei*, Berlin.

Schmaltz, B. 1983. Mensch und Tier in der griechischen Antike, in: H. Müller-Karpe (ed.), *Zur frühen Mensch-Tier-Symbiose*, München, 99–114.

Schmidt, K. 2006. *Sie bauten die ersten Tempel. Das rätselhafte Heiligtum der Steinzeitjäger*, München.

Schmidt, L. 1963. *Die Volkserzählung. Märchen – Sage – Legende – Schwank*, Berlin.

Schürmann, W. 1996. *Das Heiligtum des Hermes und der Aphrodite in Syme Viannou. II. Die Tierstatuetten aus Metall*, Athen.

Schweitzer, B. 1969. *Die geometrische Kunst Griechenlands*, Köln.

Schwendemann, K. 1921. Der Dreifuss: Ein Formen- und Religionsgeschichtlicher Versuch, *JdI* 36, 98–185.

Scullion 2007. Festivals in: D. Ogden (ed.), *A Companion to Greek Religion*, Malden–Oxford, 190–203.

Siewert, P. – J. Ebert 1999. Eine archaische Bronzeurkunde aus Olympia mit Vorschriften für Ringkämpfer und Kampfrichter, in: A. Mallwitz – K. Herrmann (eds), *XI. Bericht über die Ausgrabungen in Olympia*, Berlin, 391–412.

Siewert, P. 1991. Staatliche Weihungen von Kesseln und anderen Bronzegeräten in Olympia, *AM* 106, 81–84.

Simon, E. 1998. *Die Götter der Griechen*, München.

Sinn, U. 1981. Das Heiligtum der Artemis Limnatis bei Kombothekra, *AM* 96, 25–71.

Sinn, U. 1991. Olympia. Die Stellung der Wettkämpfe im Kult des Zeus Olympios, *Nikephoros* 4, 31–54.

Sinn, U. 2000. Olympia, in: *DNP* Vol. 8, 1170–1184.

Sinn, U. 2004. *Das antike Olympia. Götter, Spiel und Kunst*. München.

Sinn, U. 2010. Olympia – Zeustempel und Wettkampfstätte, in E. Stein-Hölkeskamp – K-J. Hölkeskamp (Hrsg.), *Die griechische Welt. Erinnerungsorte der Antike*, München, 79–97.

Slater, W. J. 1989. Pelops at Olympia, *GRBS* 30, 485–501.

Snodgrass, A. M. 1980. *Archaic Greece. The Age of Experiment,* Berkeley.

Snodgrass, A. M. 1986. Interaction by Design: The Greek City State, in C. Renfrew (ed.), *Peer polity interaction and socio-political change*, Cambridge, 47–58.

Snodgrass, A. M. 1987. *An archaeology of Greece. The present state and future scope of a discipline*, Berkeley

Solima, I. 2011. *Heiligtümer der Artemis auf der Peloponnes,* Heidelberg.

Sommer, F. 1934. *Aḫḫijavāfrage und Sprachwissenschaft* (Abhandlungen der Bayerischen Akademie der Wissenschaften, Philosophisch-Historische Abteilung: Neue Folge 9) München.

Spence, I. G. 1993. *The cavalry of classical Greece,* Oxford.

Stasinopoulou-Kakarouga, E. 1997. Oineus I, *LIMC* Vol. VIII Suppl. 915–919.

Stein-Hölkeskamp, E. 1989. *Adelskultur und Polisgesellschaft. Studien zum griechischen Adel in archaischer und klassischer Zeit*, Stuttgart.

Sternberg, L. 1905. Die Religion der Giljaken, *Archiv für Religionswissenschaft* 8, 244–456.

Swaddling, J. 1980. *The Ancient Olympic Games*. London.

Taita, J. 2009. Fattori geografici e sviluppi cultuali. Il caso di Olimpia, in: E. Olshausen – V. Sauer (Hrsg.), *Die Landschaft und die Religion*, Stuttgart, 375–388.

Tambornino, J. 1930. Marpessa, *RE* XIV,2, 1916–1918.

Thompson, S. 1958. *Motif-index of folk-literature: a classification of narrative elements in folktales, ballads, myths, fables, medieval romances, exempla, fabliaux, jest-books, and local legends*. Bloomington 1955–1958.

Trümpy, H. 1950. *Kriegerische Fachausdrücke im griechischen Epos. Untersuchungen zum Wortschatze Homers,* Basel.

Tsountas, Chr. 1892. Εκ του Αμυκλαιου, *AEphem* 2–31.

Uhsadel-Gülke, Chr. 1972. *Knochen und Kessel* (Beiträge zur klassischen Philologie Bd. 43) Meisenheim.

Ulf, Ch. / Weiler, I. 1980. Der Ursprung der antiken olympischen Spiele in der Forschung, *Stadion* 6, 1–38.

Ulf, Chr. 1997a. Die Mythen um Olympia – politischer Gehalt und politische Intention, *Nikephoros* 10, 9–51.

Ulf, Ch. 1997b. Überlegungen zur Funktion überregionaler Feste im archaischen Griechenland, in W. Eder – K.-J. Hölkeskamp (ed.), *Volk und Verfassung im vorhellenistischen Griechenland*, Stuttgart, 37–61.

Usener, H. 1913. Göttliche Synonyme, in idem, *Kleine Schriften IV. Arbeiten zur Religionsgeschichte*, Leipzig, 259 – 306 (originally published: *Rhein. Mus.* 53, 1898, 329–379).

Vallois, R. 1926. Les origins des jeux olympiques I: La course des Dactyles et Dèmèter Chamyne, *Revue des Études Anciennes* 28, 305–322.

van Vuure, C. 2005. *Retracing the aurochs: history, morphology and ecology of an extinct wild ox*, Sofia.

Vernant, J-P. 1979. Manger aux pays du Soleil, in: M. Détienne – J-P. Vernant, *La cuisine du sacrifice en pays grec*, Paris, 239–250.

Versnel, H. S. 1993. *Inconsistencies in Greek and Roman religion II. Transition and reversal in myth and ritual*, Leiden.

von Bothmer, D. 1950. *Greek, Etruscan and Roman Antiquities from the Collection of Walter Cummings Baker*, New York.

von Kamptz, H. 1982. *Homerische Personennamen. Sprachwissenschaftliche und historische Klassifikation*. Göttingen.

von Lengerken, H. 1955. *Ur, Hausrind und Mensch*, Berlin.

von Reden, S. 2010. *Money in Classical Antiquity*, Cambridge.

Voyatzis, M. E. 1990, *The early sanctuary of Athena Alea at Tegea and other archaic sanctuaries in Arcadia,* Göteborg.

Weber, M. 1971. Die geometrischen Dreifusskessel, *AM* 86, 13–30.

Weiler, I. 1974. *Der Agon im Mythos*. Darmstadt.

Weniger, G-Ch. (ed.) 1999. *Archäologie und Biologie des Auerochsen*, Neanderthal Museum.

Weniger, L. 1895. *Der heilige Ölbaum in Olympia*, Weimar.

Weniger, L. 1905. Das Hochfest des Zeus in Olympia: Olympische Zeitenordnung, *Klio* 5, 28–65.

Weniger, L. 1907. Artemisdienst in Olympia und Umgebung, *Neue Jahrbücher für das Klassische Altertum* 19, 96–114.

Weniger, L. 1915. Die Seher von Olympia, *Archiv für Religionswissenschaft* 18, 53–115.

Weniger, L. 1919. *Altgriechischer Baumkultus*, Leipzig.

Wide, S. 1893. *Lakonische Kulte*, Leipzig.

Wilamowitz, U. von 1922. *Pindaros,* Berlin.

Willemsen, F. 1957. *Dreifusskessel von Olympia* (OlForsch 3), Berlin.

Willetts, R. F. 1955. *Aristocratic Society in Ancient Crete*, London.

Ziehen, L. 1939. Olympia, in: RE XVIII.1, 2–71.

Zimmermann, J- L. 1989. *Les chevaux de bronze dans l'art géometrique grec*, Mainz.

Zografou, A. 2005. Images et "reliques" en Grece ancienne. L'omoplate de Pélops, in: Ph. Borgeaud and Y. Volokhine (eds), *Les Objets de la mémoire: pour une approche comparatiste des reliques et de leur culte*, Bern, 123–145.

Index of Ancient Passages Cited

Achilleus Tatios
   7.13: 66 n. 196

[Apollodoros]
   Bibliotheke
      1.59–60: 80 n. 250
      2.169–180: 18 n. 31, 98
      3.28: 89
   Epitome
      1.9: 86 n. 284

[Aristoteles]
   Athenaion Politeia
      54.7: 67 n. 202
   Historia Animalium
      575b.5: 73 n. 228
      499a.4: 111 n. 360
   Mirabilia
      842b33: 111

Arnobius
   4.25: 82 n. 246

Artemidoros
   4.4: 66 n. 196

Athenaios
   4.141e–f: 17

Bacchylides
   fr. 61: 78 n. 245

Caesar
   Bellum Gallicum
      6.22: 111-112

Clemens Alexandrinus
   Protrepticus
      4.47.6: 82 n. 246

Dionysios of Halicarnassus
   7.72.3: 63 n. 184

Diodoros Siculus
   3.66: 86 n. 287
   5.32: 70 n. 219, 74 n. 230
   5.79.1: 86 n. 284
   11.26.7: 29 n. 83
   14.17.8: 89 n. 298

Ephoros
   fr. 149: 54 n. 150, 62

Euripides
   Bacchae: 86 n. 285

Firmicus Maternus
   De errore prof. relig.
      15.1-2: 82 n. 246

Herodotos
   1.46–49: 30 n. 84
   1.59: 23 n. 48
   2.53: 85
   3.97: 70 n. 219
   4.30: 56 n. 159, 76 n. 237
   4.94: 70 n. 219
   6.87: 67 n. 202
   7.208: 18 n. 30
   7.126: 50 n. 142, 110
   9.33: 30 n. 86

Hesychios
   karneatai: 18 n. 32
   agetes: 19

Homeros
   Iliad

2.104–105: 84
2.402–403: 73 n. 227
7.313–315: 73 n. 227
11. 670–761: 35 n. 99, 40
11. 699–704: 26 n. 67, 55
11.725-730: 55
12. 22–23: 50 n. 141
23. 257–897: 25
23. 626–650: 26

Odyssey
3. 274: 53 n. 148
4. 602: 53 n. 148
16. 295–296: 50 n. 141
12. 347: 52
19. 420–423: 73 n. 227
21. 347: 54 n. 151

Hyginus
84: 78 n. 245, 80 n. 253
85: 78 n. 244
185: 78 n. 245, 80 n. 253

Livius
27.32.9: 35 n. 99

Martialis
1.104.8: 111 n. 359

Pausanias
1.44.1: 63 n. 184
2.28.2-3: 64
2.32.10: 65, 81 n. 256
2.34.2: 84 n. 272
3.1: 84 n. 273
3.13.3-4: 18 n. 31, 85 n. 270, 98
3.13.5: 95-96
3.14.2: 84 n. 273
3.16.11: 65 n. 190
3.22.12: 99 n. 323

5.1.9: 35 n. 99
5. 3-4: 18 n. 31
5.5.2: 56 n. 159, 76 n. 237
5.6.6: 59 n. 172, 65, 71 n. 222
5.7.9: 67
5.7.10 – 5.8.5: 11 n. 3
5.8.2: 82 n. 259
5.8.5: 11, 18 n. 31
5. 8.6 – 5. 9.6: 67 n. 201
5.8.7: 70
5.10.4: 29 n. 83
5.13.2: 88
5.13.4–7: 82 n. 264
5.13.5: 83
5.13.7: 84 n. 272
5.13.8: 126
5.13.11: 65, 72 n. 224
5.14.2: 64 n. 189
5.14.6: 65
5.14.10: 13 n. 11
5.15.4–7: 13 n. 11, 65 n. 192
5.16.1: 13 n. 12, 125
5.18.8: 13 n. 11, 65 n. 192
5.20.1: 68 n. 205
5.20.9: 13 n. 11
5.21–25: 24 n. 55
6.10.3: 84 n. 272
6.20.2: 13 n. 11
6.20.7: 78 n. 244
6.20.9: 65 n. 193
6.22.1: 80
6.22.8: 65
6.26.1-2: 86 n. 286
7.19.1-6: 66 n. 197
7.26.5: 66 n. 197
8.13.2: 65 n. 190
8.14.5-6: 55 n. 157
8.35.8: 65
10.9.3-4: 40 n. 117

10.13.1-4: 111 n. 359
10.13.9: 29 n. 83

Philostratos
Gymn. 5: 15
Vita Apollonii 6.24: 111 n. 360

Phlegon
fr. 1: 63 n.186, 67 n. 204

Pindaros
Ol. 3. 19: 61 n. 176
Ol. 3. 35: 69
Ol. 6. 6: 13 n. 13, 30 n. 86
Isthm. 3/4. 70–71: 78 n. 245

Plinius, *Naturalis Historia*
8.38: 112-113
16.69: 95 n. 316
28.34: 82 n. 264

Plutarchos
Agis 11.3: 69 n. 215
Aristeides 21: 67 n. 202
Lykourgos 1: 67 n. 204
Moralia 293 C: 69 n. 215
299 B: 82 n. 263
299 E-F: 87 n. 289
303 B: 56 n. 159
364 F: 82 n. 263

Polybios
4.73: 35 n. 99

Scylax
94: 83 n. 270

Sophokles
fr. 432: 78 n. 245

Strabo
5.1.9: 55 n. 157
5.4.7: 67 n. 202
7.7.6: 67 n. 202
8.3.12: 71 n. 222, 72
8.3.30: 18 n. 31, 29, 36 n. 103
10.4.20-21: 54 n. 150, 62
13.2.5: 83 n. 270
16.4.9: 111 n. 360
17.1.10: 67 n. 202

Thukydides
1.6.5: 63
1.9: 83
3. 88: 84 n. 271
3.104: 67 n. 202
5.54: 18 n. 30
5.75: 18 n. 30

Tyrtaios
fr.2 (Bergk): 83, 85

Vergilius
Georgica 2.374: 112

Xenophon
Anab. 5.3.8-11: 59 n. 172, 65, 71 n. 222
Hell. 3.2.26: 35 n. 99

varia
Anecdota Graeca (ed. I. Bekker)
1. 305: 18 n.27
Etymologicum Magnum s.v. Elis
(p. 426): 127 n. 386
Genesis 18: 86
22: 85
Kypria, fr. 16.3-4 (West):
83 n. 269

Scholia in
    Pind. Ol. 1.127: 89 n. 298
    Pind. Ol. 3.35a: 17 n. 23, 19 n. 36,
        69 n. 213
    Pind. Ol. 3.35d: 61 n.176
    Pind. Ol. 6.6: 13 n. 13, 29
    Pind. Isthm. 4. 92a: 78 n. 245
    Plat. Phaedr. 231e: 15 n. 20
    Plat. Phaedr. 236 b3: 71 n.220
    Theokritos 5. 83b: 19
    Theokritos 4.7: 65 n.191

Edited by
ERZSÉBET JEREM and WOLFGANG MEID

Main Series

27. **The Medieval Royal Palace at Visegrád.** Edited by Gergely Buzás and József Laszlovszky. 2013. 398 pp. € 66.-. ISBN 978-963-9911-39-0.
28. **Explorations in Salt Archaeology in the Carpathian Zone.** Edited by Anthony Harding and Valerii Kavruk. 2013. 332. pp. € 60.-. ISBN 978-963-9911-44-4.
29. **Textiles from Hallstatt / Textilien aus Hallstatt. Weaving Culture in Bronze Age and Iron Age Salt Mines / Gewebte Kultur aus dem bronze- und eisenzeitlichen Salzbergwerk (bilingual).** Edited by Karina Grömer, Anton Kern, Hans Reschreiter and Helga Rösel-Mautendorfer. 2013. 572 pp. € 65.-. ISBN 978-963-9911-46-8.
30. **Transitions to the Bronze Age. Interregional Interaction and Socio-Cultural Change in the Third Millennium BC Carpathian Basin and Neighbouring Regions.** Edited by Volker Heyd, Gabriella Kulcsár and Vajk Szeverényi. 2013. 358 pp. € 60.-. ISBN 978-963-9911-48-2.
31. Paul R. Duffy: **Complexity and Autonomy in Bronze Age Europe. Assessing Cultural Developments in Eastern Hungary.** 2014. 402 pp. € 60.-. ISBN 978-963-9911-52-9
32. **The Medieval Royal Town at Visegrád. Royal Centre, Urban Settlement, Churches.** Edited by Buzás Gergely, Laszlovszky József and Mészáros Orsolya. 2014. 272 pp. € 40.-. ISBN 978-963-9911-58-1.
33. **Aspects of the Design, Production and Use of Textiles and Clothing from the Bronze Age to the Early Modern Era. NESAT XII. The North European Symposium of Archaeological Textiles 21st – 24th May 2014 in Hallstatt, Austria.** Edited by Karina Grömer and Frances Pritchard. 2015. 374 pp. € 64.-. ISBN 978-963-9911-67-3.
34. Attila Gyucha: **Prehistoric Village Social Dynamics. The Early Copper Age in the Körös Region.** 2015. 352 pp. € 54.-. ISBN 978-963-9911-68-0.
35. **Persistent Economic Ways of Living. Production, Distribution, and Consumption in Late Prehistory and Early History.** Edited by Alžběta

Danielisová and Manuel Fernández-Götz. 2015. 243 pp. € 50.-. ISBN 978-963-9911-70-3.

Series Minor

1. Wolfgang Meid: **Gaulish Inscriptions. Their interpretation in the light of archaeological evidence and their value as a source of linguistic and sociological information.** 2014. (Third edition, revised and enlarged) 74 pp. € 20.-. ISBN 978-963-9911-61-1.
28. Sofia Pescarin: **Reconstructing Ancient Landscape.** 2009. 264 pp. € 36.-. ISBN 978-963-9911-09-3
30. **A History of Central European Archaeology.** Edited by Alexander Gramsch and Ulrike Sommer. 2011. 219 pp. € 24.-. ISBN 978-963-9911-23-9.
31. **Archaeological Imaginations of Religion.** Edited by Thomas Meier and Petra Tillessen. 2014. 404 pp. € 38.-. ISBN 978-963-9911-24-6.
32. Mária Bondár: **Prehistoric Wagon Models in the Carpathian Basin.** 2012. 142 pp. € 20.-. ISBN 978-963-9911-34-5.
33. **Appropriate narratives. Archaeologists, publics and stories.** Edited by Elisabeth Niklasson and Thomas Meier. 2013. 298 pp. € 34.-. ISBN 978-963 9911-47-5.
34. Alexander Falileyev: **In Search of the Eastern Celts. Studies in Geographical Names, their Distribution and Morphology.** 2014. 173 pp. € 28.-. ISBN 978-963-9911-56-7.
35. Magdolna Szilágyi: **On the Road: The History and Archaeology of Medieval Communication Networks in East-Central Europe.** 2014. 250 pp. € 36.-. ISBN 978-963-9911-57-4.
36. Gábor Ilon: **The Golden Treasure from Szent Vid in Velem. The Costume of a High-Ranking Lady of the Late Bronze Age in the Light of New Studies.** 2015. ca. 260 pp. € 36.-. ISBN 978-963-9911-71-0.

Please address orders to:

ARCHAEOLINGUA

H-1250 Budapest, Pf. 41.
Fax: (+361) 3758939
e-mail: kovacsr@archaeolingua.hu
http://www.archaeolingua.hu   www.hungarianarchaeology.hu